Please pra...
Dr & Mrs. Alton Robb...

THE PROBLEM OF EVIL

IS VOLUME

20

OF THE

Twentieth Century Encyclopedia of Catholicism

UNDER SECTION

II

THE BASIC TRUTHS

IT IS ALSO THE

25TH

VOLUME IN ORDER OF PUBLICATION

Edited by HENRI DANIEL-ROPS of the Académie Française

THE PROBLEM OF EVIL

By FRANÇOIS PETIT, O. Praem

Translated from the French by CHRISTOPHER WILLIAMS

HAWTHORN BOOKS · PUBLISHERS · *New York*

First Edition, September, 1959

NIHIL OBSTAT

Hubertus Richards, S.T.L., L.S.S.

Censor Deputatus

IMPRIMATUR

E. Morrogh Bernard

Vicarius Generalis

Westmonasterii, die VI MAII MCMLIX

CONTENTS

INTRODUCTION

The problem of evil has already been dealt with often enough from very different angles. There is no theologian, philosopher or author of apologetics, indeed no writer worthy of the name, who has not been confronted with this question. It cannot be avoided. The metaphysician searches for the elements of a solution solely in the principles of human reason and in our natural knowledge of God. The psychologist studies the repercussions of evil in the human mind and in the feelings which are its expression, in the organization of life and in ordinary behaviour. More often than from any other point of view it has been studied from that of apologetics. This problem constitutes one of the great difficulties of faith. It is therefore of the utmost importance that it should be shown that the existence of evil is compatible not only with the existence of God, but also with God's love for us, which is the central point of our faith. "We have learned to recognize the love God has in our regard, to recognize it, and to make it our belief" (1 John 4. 16).

In this series we have to study evil in the framework of theology. After listing the human solutions and the sources of revelation, we shall devote a third section to their synthetic elaboration. That is the proper work of theology, the rational systematization of the data of revealed truth. It cannot be pretended that this is anything but the most fragile part of the discussion, the least enduring, since the requirements of human reason vary considerably from age to age, from one culture, one country, to another. Finally, because of the intimate relation between moral and dogmatic truth, a fourth section will study the practical consequences of Christian teaching about evil and suffering.

As the problem of evil is insoluble apart from ideas of the Fall, redemption, glorification and ascetical life, this volume will prove to be in its own fashion a brief summary of Christian doctrine. Thus evil, which is by itself an absence of being, becomes, by the void that it creates, an appeal to God and to the divine action. A provisional, but valid and complete, solution to this problem can be given by repeating the words sung by the deacon in the Easter Vigil: *O felix culpa quae talem ac tantum meruit habere Redemptorem!* "O happy fault to win for us so great and so mighty a Redeemer!"

Mondaye Abbey
June 30th, 1957

PART I

HUMAN SOLUTIONS

CHAPTER I

EVIL: A PROBLEM OR A

MYSTERY?

For every thinking and reflecting man the existence of evil is a riddle he cannot escape. The world as a whole, in virtue of the order and beauty which fill it, seems to us to be the work of a wonderful intelligence which has organized it all. The marvels which we discover every day in the universe, both in the infinitely large things and in the infinitely small, as well as the newly-acquired techniques for governing the lower orders of creation and making them serve our needs, give added strength to this impression. In short, the world appears intelligible. But it is at this point that we meet, in a twofold form, what we call evil: we find suffering in the world, and sometimes cruel suffering, physical or mental. On the other hand, we realize soon enough that some at least of these sufferings are the result of wrong that has been done, that is, of a disorder introduced voluntarily, by a free decision, into the divine handiwork. We experience the fact of sin and suffering and a relationship between them which it will be our task to define. This is why so many people are provoked to ask, "How can God allow all this?" Or again, "If God existed, should we be seeing all this?"

At times, too, a certain uneasiness comes over us: a group of people or things are not what they ought to be. We compare the idea we normally have of them with the realization of those ideas which we actually experience. There is dislocation, and that in all the beings of the world of human experience. This provokes us, hurts us, makes us suffer. In whatever manner, it is not long before we are confronted with this problem.

We shall see what solutions can be found. Some of them, on days when we feel calm and contented, seem to satisfy us well enough. At other times, when physical or mental suffering becomes acute, the theoretical solutions seem poor and insufficient. Is it in fact true that suffering and evil are inexplicable? Do they contain a mystery, properly so called? Not exactly, not in the same way as the other mysteries. The Trinity, the Incarnation are known to us only through revelation. They arouse insoluble problems in our minds. Revelation and theological reflection throw a little light on the terms of the inexplicable proposition, show us its appropriateness, its splendour, and disclose the riches it can bring to the spiritual life. Here, on the contrary, the disturbing antinomy comes to light of itself, without needing to be revealed: why is there evil in a world which, as a whole, seems good? We know the terms only too well, but find it hard to make out their ultimate explanation. The Judaeo-Christian revelation casts a deep, gentle, calming glow of light over the data of the case, but does not illuminate them perfectly. For one who suffers, kissing a crucifix is not a clear and definitive solution of the problem, but it is a consolation which goes beyond the suffering itself, where the correct and plausible explanations provided by philosophy would fail to bring him peace.

It is thus that one can say that evil constitutes at once a problem and a mystery: a problem, because on reflection it comes to light of itself before the arrival of any revelation, a mystery because faith can illuminate it in a way that is useful but which in this world must remain incomplete. Only, while the Trinity and the Incarnation will preserve their mysterious character when we contemplate their splendour in heaven, it may be that the existence of evil will then no longer present a difficulty.

Let us add that it is even harder for the Christian to set aside the problem of evil than it is for the philosopher who lacks the faith. The latter can always use the device of telling himself that perhaps he is mistaken in believing the world to be intelligible. The former, with his belief in the infinite wisdom and goodness of God, cannot shirk the question. He knows with an inescapable certainty that creation is good because every being derives its existence from God, because what is evil in itself cannot come from the hands of the Creator. The riddle is at once painful and urgent. We must try hard to get a clear view of it.

CHAPTER II

MYTHICAL EXPLANATIONS

In point of time the first explanation of evil is given us by myths, symbolic stories, popular traditions, taken up with a constantly deepening vision and intensity of feeling by the epic, lyric and tragic poets. The story of Prometheus stealing the heavenly fire from the gods to give it to men, of the giants piling Pelion on Ossa to climb up to attack Olympus, and of Pandora's box, are all examples of this. Plato in the *Timaeus* tells the story of the origin of evil in the following way: God, being good and without envy, wished everything that composed the universe to be good, to be as far as possible like himself. But after forming the gods, a shining and beautiful race, made almost exclusively of fire, he charged them with the formation of the other races by mixing mortal substance with immortal. This was the source of failure and error.[1]

[1] The author of all this says to them: "Gods of the gods, the works of which I am maker and father are indestructible unless I will, since they proceed from me.... Hear now the things I have to say to you and show you. Three mortal races still remain unborn. Until these are born heaven will be incomplete, since it will not contain within itself every race of living beings, as it should, if it is to reach full perfection. If they receive their birth and their share of life from me they will be equals of the gods. In order, therefore, that they may be mortal, and this universe really whole and entire, do you set about the formation of living beings in accordance with your nature, imitating the power I displayed in giving you your birth. It is fitting that there should be in them an element which shares the name of the immortal, which is called divine, and which gives the lead to those amongst them who in each generation consent to live justly and to

From Persian sources we have another dualist explanation. Monotheism, the religion of a sole deity opposed by the forces of evil, has degenerated into a new theology, in which good and evil have become two perpetually opposing forces, both of equal reality, vowed to a struggle which can only end in victory or defeat.

A third myth, which has permeated the thought of India, might be added. It is an extreme pessimism by which all evil is attributed to activity. Hence the obligation of an indefinitely repeated rebirth after death, to expiate the wrong done by action, all the more so if this action has been, properly speaking, wicked. Buddhism aims at drawing the individual out of this flux and making him cross the stream until he arrives at the other bank whence there is no returning; it is achieved by a rupture with egoism, by ceasing to have desires, by letting the influence of activity die away without renewal and leads to a supreme confidence in the value of asceticism and exact knowledge.

These three myths are found again and again in the history of philosophy. They all contain an element of truth: the perfection of the universe demands the existence of imperfect beings, the revolt of creatures against their Creator has produced disorder, lastly there is a solidarity which pervades all generations, making the younger bear the punishment of those who have gone before.

follow you. This element I will beget and inaugurate and then entrust to you. For the rest, you yourselves by weaving what is mortal into what is immortal shall fashion living beings, bring them to birth, give them nourishment that they may grow, and when they die receive them back to yourselves. (Plato, *Timaeus* 41a5–d3.)

CHAPTER III

PHILOSOPHICAL

EXPLANATIONS

For lack of the idea of a divine government of the universe, the first philosophers did not approach the problem of evil as we do. For Socrates, as for Plato, wrongdoing is to a large extent confused with ignorance. It is much less a moral evil than a natural deficiency. Aristotle, who thought of God as drawing the world to himself in the manner of final causes, had no idea of Providence. For him the existence of evil could not be a stumbling-block. Although he maintained the principle of freedom against Socrates and Plato, he made no attempt to explain responsibility. The Stoics suppressed the problem by denying evil, regarding pain as nothing more than a word. Alternatively, they attributed it entirely to man. The wise man, the *sapiens*, should attain to impassibility. Should the world collapse, its ruins might crush him and he would not be afraid. Epicurus himself believed there was a way of arriving at happiness with a minimum of exterior goods by reducing one's demands and one's wants.

Greek wisdom, nevertheless, believed in the goodness of the world, though without any self-complacency. Epictetus and Marcus Aurelius had no illusions about their suffering, even if they deliberately ignored it. In contrast with this we find the following conception of the universe. Since one of the most important discoveries of philosophy was the distinction between spirit and matter, on account of the imperfection of material nature and the sufferings it brings, there was a great temptation to identify matter with evil, good with spirit. This is the attitude of *Gnosticism*. The world, including the heavenly bodies, is on this view wholly bad, it is the fullness, the *pleroma*, of evil. While the Stoic *sapiens* paid little attention to his personal destiny, however painful, so that he might sink himself in the general harmony of the cosmos, the Gnostic took great care of his own salvation. How was he to escape from this evil world? Instead of being deliberately optimistic like the *sapiens*, he is deliberately pessimistic in the face of cosmic evil, for it is the stars themselves that impose on the soul its imperfections and vices.

Where can the Gnostic find refuge? Nowhere but in God. His idea of God, borrowed no doubt from Jewish revelation, is very lofty. It is expressed by two words which indicate its infinite separation from matter and the clamour of material beings: God is the great Silence and the Abyss. He is to be sought above the stars. No consideration of the world can help to find him, because the world is evil. We have to wait for revelation. This higher knowledge, *gnosis*, is man's salvation, only to be won by piety.

If God is good and the world evil, how can the existence of the world be explained? The Judaeo-Christian solution— God created the world good, but the free will of creatures brought disorder into it—appeared to the Gnostic an oversimplification. The only way out, he believed, was to attribute the creation of the world to another than God, to the demiurge. Between God and this demiurge Gnosticism introduced a whole intermediary world composed of aeons which emanated from God in couples, male and female. In the midst of the series one aeon sinned and was excluded from the divine world. This was the demiurge, the god of the Jews, a criminal spirit who has to be resisted.

The Gnostic's whole moral attitude is therefore opposed to that of the *sapiens*. The latter is in harmony with the world, tries to improve it by doing good in his own surroundings; the former believes the world incapable of betterment. He does all he can to flee the world and return to God.

It will perhaps be objected that this is what is done by the Christian who, instead of working for a better world, retires into solitude to have time for contemplation. But the two cases are not parallel. The Christian believes that the world can and should be improved. If he retires into solitude it is because he has a particular vocation. He does not claim that every Christian ought to withdraw from the world. Moreover he is convinced that his contemplation, by the prayer it inspires and the example it gives, tends to alter the world for the better. What is more, when the fervent Christian adopts a certain ascetic practice, he does not impose it on himself as if the things from which he abstains were bad, he indicates rather that it is necessary to be able to exercise self-control in the use of things which can be excellent, but which, in excess, endanger self-possession.

Manicheism is connected with Gnosticism in so far as it too is a religion of salvation, and of a salvation based on knowledge, but its diffusion has been so extensive and the influence it has exercised, and always exercises, so great, that it is as well to give it separate consideration.

Its influence was not due to any lack of persecution and strong opposition. The Manichean scriptures disappeared from the Christian west in the sixth century, from the Byzantine east in about the ninth century, from the Islamic world in the eleventh, and from the Chinese Empire in about the fourteenth, and until 1904 the only basis on which they could be discussed was that of indirect evidence, in particular the writings of St Augustine. Discoveries in the region of Turfan (Turkestan) and Fayum (Upper Egypt) have put us in possession of part of the writings of Mani, liturgical documents and commentaries.

Mani was born in the south of Babylonia in A.D. 215. He was of royal descent. After initiation, it seems certain, in a sect which practised baptism, he left it to travel in India. Returning to Persia he preached between 242 and 276 with encouragement from the royal house. In the latter year he was accused of heresy by the clergy of the official fire-worshipping religion, imprisoned, and put in chains. He died in prison on February 14th.

His aim was to explain man to himself and thereby to save him. He did this by means of a myth which, as it is unfolded, shows the luxuriance of an oriental imagination. This myth can be clothed in Persian or Christian imagery, for it is in itself no more than a metaphysical explanation of the problem of evil. It could take its start either from a particular affliction or from the suffering inherent in the human condition as a whole. Man recognizes that his position is that of a stranger and a slave. He has the impression that his origin must be greatly superior to this state. He conceives a primitive, basic purity—joy, peace and freedom—defiled in actuality by the body, by the outside world, in short, by matter, to which both these belong. Hence the hypothesis that our essential self is superior to the body and the world. We can think of it as a luminous, good substance mingled with one that is dark and evil. This abnormal mixture presupposes a fall, a wrong committed, since previously the luminous substance, pure and independent, was completely separate from the darkness. Perhaps we can hope for a new separation which will restore things to their natural state.

The projection of these few statements on the cosmic plane gives the Manichean myth its grandeur. The story of man, the microcosm, becomes that of the universe or macrocosm. Two doctrines begin to be elaborated, that of two principles or two sources, Good and Evil, then that of three states: before,

during and after—the original separation, the dreadful
mingling, the return to the natural state or *apocatastasis*.

Man's salvation, and that of the world too, follows directly
from knowledge. Man, as in all Gnosticism and religions of
initiation, is his own saviour. The soul, the *psyche*, which has
fallen into matter, is delivered by *nous*, the Intellect or Knowledge. Thus, originally, in the "former time", before the dis-
astrous mingling, there existed a radical duality of two natures
or substances or sources, on the one hand light, which is also
Good and God himself, on the other darkness, Evil or matter,
which is later assimilated, in Manicheism of a Christian form,
to the devil, the Prince of darkness. But each of the two principles is so of equal right. Each is unborn and eternal. Each
has equal value and equal power. Thus from the start it is
the most realist and extreme solution of the problem of evil.
Here and there we are indeed told that light is superior to
darkness, because it is gentle, beautiful and intelligent, whereas matter is wicked, heavy and stupid, but there is a complete
equality. Possibly the very peace-loving goodness of light constitutes an inferiority when compared with the warlike violence
of darkness.

Originally the two principles were separate. But there arose
the catastrophe which inaugurated the "mediant moment".
Darkness is a force and hurls itself at light to devour it and
cause it to disappear. It is possible that the attack on the
kingdom of light by darkness corresponds with the Manicheans to a consciousness of sin, when all the dark forces of
the subconscious emerge into the region of light to occupy
and destroy it.

The whole story of the formation of the world and the
beginnings of humanity is woven out of the struggle of light
and darkness. The progress of the world shows two parallel
activities, the propagation of the evil mingling, but at the
same time the unfolding of salvation. The cosmic Jesus, whose
soul is light, is always crucified to matter. The whole world

is the cross of light. But he saves himself. This slow physical process is dragged down by the sins of humanity, in as much as men refuse to bind themselves to sexual abstinence which alone can bring about the deliverance of light and the end of the universe. When this happens, the third moment will have arrived, because the defeat of Evil will have rendered it incapable of renewing its endeavours.

The individual must reproduce in himself this *apocatastasis*, this final restoration, which for the cosmos will be definitive at the end of time. A severe negative morality, made up of rules of abstinence, enables it to be attained. Everything is condemned: wealth, property, war, hunting, commerce, agriculture; no secular activity is left. Clearly there had to be a compromise, so that the "auditors", the simple among those who heard the teaching, might be permitted to have what was refused by the "perfect". Even the "perfect" were forced to take a vegetarian meal each day. They left the sin of digging up the vegetables or plucking the fruit to the "auditors". The digestion of the "elect" or "perfect" was thought of as separating and freeing the particles of light from the vegetable matter. This was only tolerated, and frequent fasts were imposed. Salvation lay in abstaining from matter.

Manicheism, despite the rigorous character of its morality, spread rapidly. It passed from Persia to Egypt, North Africa and Palestine. It reached Rome under Pope Miltiades. It infiltrated into Gaul, Spain, Turkestan and Central Asia. It reappeared in the Bogomils, the Cathari, the Albigensians. Its mark is to be found in Pierre Bayle, John Stuart Mill, Wilfrid Monod. It constitutes a permanent temptation for many Christians, not in the sense that they make the devil the equal of God in power and dynamic force, but in the sense that through a spirit of mortification they come to consider matter as evil, and that their ascetical practice, instead of tending to the control of matter, goes no further than abstinence and refusal.

In the same epoch—for Mani and Plotinus both took part in the Persian expedition against the Emperor Gordian, but in opposing camps—Plotinus, the disciple of Ammonius Saccas and head of the Neo-Platonist school, was himself at grips with the problem of evil. All his teaching seems to have been directed against those who refuse to recognize the moral government of the world, and who thus come to attribute the universe to chance, on account of the conflicts and chaos that reign in it, or claim to find some imperfection or wickedness in God. Plotinus explains the existence of evil by the very order of the world. At the summit he sees God, the One, absolute perfection, whom abstract reasoning can never grasp, but to whom access is given by mystical contemplation. In him nothing is lacking. He can give of his perfection as the over-full vessel spills over without ceasing to be full, as the sun produces its bright rays without losing heat or light.

Beneath God comes *Intelligence*, wonderfully good, but not possessing the whole goodness of God, because it comes from God. The effect is like the cause, but it has not all its virtue.

At a lower level is placed the *World-Soul*, also eternal, but inferior to Intelligence, comprising a multiplicity of distinct elements, plastic forms by which the Soul is immediately disposed to enter into contact with our sensible world. It is less good than Intelligence, because it is of a hybrid nature, being on the frontier of spirit and matter. It gives birth to Time in producing the sensible world.

At the lower extremity of the sensible world is found Matter, pure multiplicity, which has no stability, but is pure becoming. It has no solidity, but constitutes a pure void. It preserves no intelligibility or beauty, but becomes the principle of all error and ugliness. "It is," said Plotinus, "pure potency; frequently it is not-being, the essence of untruth" (*Enneads* II, c. 10). Good is here totally wanting. With matter we reach the essence of evil.

Plotinus gives this résumé of his system: Since goodness

does not remain alone, it is necessary that evil should exist through progressive separation from goodness, that is, through the relative inferiority of beings which, proceeding one from another, set themselves further and further away from goodness. Or, if this way of speaking is preferable, evil comes into being because the divine power lowers itself and is drained away, so that in the series of successive emanations it is enfeebled step by step. There is an ultimate degree of being beyond which nothing further can be engendered. This is evil. The world, then, in its totality, is a mixture of good and evil. Above there is the One which is good without any defect; below, prime matter which *is* evil: two limits, the one all light, the other wholly darkness. However, Plotinus did not hold with Aristotle that evil is simply privation of being. For the latter prime matter is a good in potency, a good in anticipation. It is an aptitude, a tendency, for good, a capacity receptive of good. For Plotinus matter has a certain being, but an inferior being, which moreover is not convertible into good. It has not even the being which would permit it to have a share in good. There *is* a defect of being which consists in not being the supreme good (this is the condition of everything which comprises the world), but evil is the total lack of good.

For this Platonist all good is contained in the world of essences, of "Ideas". Once the contamination of matter is introduced, evil becomes present. Thus evil is eternal like God himself. The responsibility for it does not attach to the First Cause. The order of the emanations constitutes already an eternal necessity.

Against the inroads of evil the only way of resistance is conversion, that is, the ascent of the soul towards God. The first stage is the desire of resembling God. From here the soul proceeds to a turning in upon itself, an interior concentration, a purification which expresses itself in an effort of abstraction in order to become soul once more, an effort of intuition in order to become spirit once more, an effort of ecstasy in order to become once again the One. It is a rationalist piety, different enough, indeed, from Christian piety. One cannot, however, deny it a certain grandeur. We are very far from the Manichean morality. But the two conceptions join in admitting that good comes from God and evil from matter, that we better ourselves in the measure in which we are dematerialized. They are alike above all in the conviction that man must save himself, for the ecstasy of Plotinus is not a grace. It is necessarily produced when it finds the suitable preparation.

There is no philosopher who is not at some time or other confronted with the problem of evil. An analysis of their theories shows that they lead back to a larger or smaller extent to the ancient explanations. In our own days evolutionism, and above all Marxist evolutionism, by its active faith in continual progress, has reached a more or less complete identification of evil with the past and good with the future. The past stands for oppression in the realm of thought, material poverty of the workers, the future for the absorption of the whole of humanity by the working class, and thereby the disappearance of all antagonism and war. The future stands for definitive peace, in which each will find his enjoyment in devoting himself to his fellow-workers, voluntarily giving what he can, the engineer his mental work and organizing ability, the manual worker his muscular strength, in the full flowering of egalitarian justice and universal mutual help. In short, we have Paradise appearing on earth in an apocalyptic vision. For the present good and evil are mixed. The aim is to set evil in motion by class-struggle, strikes, revolutions and wars, and thus to hasten the complete overthrow of society. This theory based, as it is, on a faith—and a faith of the most imprecise kind at that—is astonishing coming from people who claim to be preeminently scientific.

More recently pessimism has had a singularly widespread revival in the existentialists of the atheist persuasion, who allege that the world is unintelligible. In this case the problem of evil is suppressed, since there is no longer any good to provide a standard of comparison. It only remains to seek to escape suffering by killing one's own desire to live.

Fr Teilhard de Chardin does not consider the world unintelligible, but thinks evil is a necessity for the evolution of the cosmos. In a world wherein progress is fortuitous or achieved by fumbling, the law of great numbers leads inevitably to an evil of disorder and failure. To this is added an evil of decay and death in the measure in which, for living beings, death has become the regular and indispensable condition of the renewal of the individual; an evil of loneliness and grief arising from the fact that human consciousness awakens to reflection in a world full of obscurity: finally an evil of growth, all progress towards unity being expressed in terms of toil and effort.

Pain and wrongdoing, blood and tears, are so many by-products (often, in fact, valuable and capable of further use), bred on the way by *Noogenesis*. Speaking only as a philosopher, the author leaves the theologian the task of seeing if a certain inexplicable excess of evil does not postulate some catastrophe or primordial deviation.

Whatever the value of these explanations, they carry little weight in face of the depths of sufferings in which the hearts of certain men and women struggle. Those explanations which have enjoyed a lasting success—Manicheism, Neo-Platonism, even Communism—have plainly taken a religious turn. Evidently, when confronted with the problem of evil, men wish to be sustained by a faith and a hope. A merely rational knowledge does not provide anything to which they can give a genuine allegiance. They have to realize that they are loved by the very power which permits suffering, and that suffering becomes for them an occasion for proving their love. With ever-increasing clarity this is shown by the features of the Judaeo-Christian revelation which we have now to examine.

PART II

THE DATA OF REVELATION

CHAPTER IV

THE OLD TESTAMENT

God's light illuminates the mystery of evil. But we must not expect it to make a sudden appearance. As Anselm, Bishop of Havelberg, and a Premonstratensian, said in the twelfth century, God works in the world after the manner of schoolmasters and doctors (*paedagogice et medicinaliter*). Revelation came only gradually.

It seems that the first truth to be revealed was the relation of dependence between suffering and moral evil, that is, sin. That in God's creation suffering does not come in the last resort from misfortune, still less from the anger of gods whose appetite sacrifices have failed to satisfy, but is rather the consequence of creatures' rebellion against God—all this seems elementary and obvious even to a child. In reality this is not so. It needed the work of many prophets and the reflection of many thinkers to convince Israel of this truth, and even today it is by no means easy to make this message understood.

Among the books of the Bible is a group of works which Hebrew scholars designate by the name "earlier prophets". These are Josue, Judges and the books of Samuel and Kings. We are inclined to regard them as historical books but in reality they are prophetical. They are "history-preaching". Their aim is to show that for Israel loyalty to the Lord is the condition of her material and moral prosperity, and that whenever Israel breaks the covenant into which God has entered with her she necessarily brings misery on herself.

The book of Judges particularly emphasizes this idea. From a whole succession of events a monotonous and melancholy rhythm emerges. In the first place, disloyalty: "Then, once again, Israel defied the Lord's will" (Judges 3. 12). In the second place they decide to run to God their saviour for help: "And now they cried out to the Lord" (*ibid*. 3. 15). In the third place: "And he sent them a fresh champion" (*ibid*.) These champions have received from posterity the name of Judges. They are often disconcerting figures, sometimes of a bloodthirsty disposition. They belong to their age. Their conscience is not yet very refined, but all have a lively faith in the living God, they obey his commands blindly, and even the succession of crises leads Israel to realize that happiness lies in loyalty to the Lord and misfortune in abandoning the law of God. The lesson is continued in the books of Samuel and Kings. The rejection of Saul, following his act of disobedience, the blessing bestowed on David because of his loyalty to God, the disasters which overwhelm the kingdoms of Israel and Juda are not referred to political causes, to the more or less able and perspicacious, or more or less faulty character of this or that monarch, but always solely to loyalty to God or sin committed against him. This rudimentary teaching left room for more precise statements in time to come, but it was necessary first of all to make this idea take firm root in the mind of the people of God—the idea that there is fundamentally only one evil, that of sin. All other evil is only the consequence, however far removed, of sin.

The first prophetic authors are filled with this idea. The primary sin of Israel is ingratitude. This people had been the object of a unique love; Israel was, as it were, the spouse of Yahweh, picked up from the gutter, raised up, loved, wonderfully adorned, but she has prostituted herself to all the other gods: "Blame her, blame your mother, that she is no true wife of mine, nor I any longer her Lord" (Osee 2. 2). Therefore she can expect every sort of misery. "I shall leave her desolate as the barren waste, the trackless desert, to die of thirst" (*ibid*. 2. 3).

But sin against the Lord has led her to all sorts of other wrongdoing. She has trampled right and justice under her feet. She has abandoned herself to a life of ease:

And this too: What of Israel?
Thrice forfeit Israel like the rest,
And forfeit once again,
That for a debt, though it were but the price of a pair of shoes,
Will make slaves of poor, honest folk.
Ground in the dust, the poor man's rights,
Shouldered aside, the claim of the unbefriended!
See where father and son, to my name's dishonour,
Bed with one maid!
...Henceforth, you shall seek my help in vain;
Waggon-axle overladen with sheaves
Groans not so reluctant as I!
Speed shall be no profit to the speedy,
Strength to the strong;
Warrior shall not escape, nor bowman stand firm.

(Amos 2. 6–7, 13–15)

So that Israel may return to God, she must first lose all her human supports: "I will lead you into a desert world, and there plead my cause against you. ... I will force you under my sceptre, chain you to my covenant. The rebels I will set apart" (Ezechiel 20. 35–8). This is the meaning of the exile. It might be said that it is the meaning of all the suffering that men experience.

About the same time the ancient tradition which had been preserved orally for several centuries, took form, and gave place to two accounts, one Jahwist, the other Elohist, called thus after the name they give to God. The older, the Jahwist, account belongs perhaps to the time of Solomon, the Elohist appears to be of a somewhat later date. Both tell of the origins of Israel, but they insert, both of them, in their narrative the laws given by God to Moses. It is fundamentally the same message: "If thou wilt listen to [the] warnings [of my angel], and do all I bid thee then thy enemies shall find an enemy in me, and those who shew thee no mercy shall find me merciless" (Exod. 23. 22).

Somewhat later, after the fall of the northern kingdom, there appeared the Deuteronomist, who certainly represents fundamentally the tradition brought by the Levites of the tribes of Israel when they took refuge at Jerusalem. The formulas are here plainer still:

> And if you obey the commands I am giving you now, by loving the Lord and serving him, heart and soul, then he will send your land rain in autumn, rain in spring, to give you a harvest of wheat, and wine, and oil; your beasts will have grass to graze on in the countryside, and you food to your heart's content. But do not let your hearts be led away into forsaking the Lord your God, and enslaving yourselves to alien worship; or the Lord, in his anger, will shut the doors of heaven; no rain will fall, earth will yield no crops, and soon the fair land the Lord means to make yours will know you no longer.
>
> (Deut. 11. 13–17)

The same idea occurs again and again throughout the book. Notably it fills the twenty-seventh and twenty-eighth chapters which describe in detail the blessings and curses sanctioning the religious and moral conduct of Israel. The lawgiver concludes: "I call heaven and earth to witness this day that I have set such a choice before thee, life or death, a blessing or a curse. Wilt thou not choose life, long life for thyself and for those that come after thee? Wilt thou not learn to love the Lord thy God, and obey him, and keep close to his side?" (Deut. 30. 19–20).

It is above all the third chapter of Genesis, of Jahwist authorship, which insists on the connection between wrongdoing and suffering. The world had left God's hands entirely good. The account of the creation, which comes from a source drawn up a little later, the priestly source, returns to the point again and again: "And God saw all that he had made, and found it very good" (Genesis 1. 31).

But God could not ordain that the creature should not *be* a creature, in absolute dependence on himself, and, since he had given man reason, had made him "wearing our own image and likeness" (Genesis 1. 26), man must needs accept and recognize this dependence. Hence a peremptory law: "Thou mayest eat thy fill of all the trees in the garden except the tree which brings knowledge of good and evil; if ever thou eatest of this, thy doom is death" (Gen. 2. 16, 17.).

The account does not attempt to explain the origin of evil to us, for it does not say where the serpent comes from, but it shows us very clearly, with a psychology truly remarkable for so distant an age, what is the nature of sin, and how it involves ruin and suffering for man.

The serpent insinuates a doubt into Eve's heart: "What is this command God has given you, not to eat the fruit of any tree in the garden?" (Gen. 3. 1). Every sin comes always from a weakening—or from a distraction—of the faith by which we are established in God's light. This light must first grow dim before the will can go astray. What is more, all sin is an attempt to make oneself God, an act of *hubris*: "and you yourselves will be like gods, knowing good and evil" (Gen. 3. 5). Even if it does not derive from megalomania, from the intoxication of pride, to sin is always to imitate the divine independence, to seek one's own glory rather than God's glory (*cf.* John 12. 43), to wish to make one's own life instead of receiving it from God's hand. That is the first, the fundamental, evil. And from this evil all the others flow. Adam and Eve become aware of their nakedness, having lost the innocence of their mutual relationship. They run away from the face of God; for God's light, which is a joy to the just, is a devouring fire for the sinner.

And the break with God brings with it disorder in man's relations with everything else. The creation which should be subordinate to man rebels against him. He will have to re-conquer it by a great struggle, with the sweat of his brow. Woman, whom God had created to be man's glory, becomes his slave and his plaything. Pain henceforth leaves its mark upon all the paths of mankind. Adam and Eve are driven out of God's garden, Cain becomes his brother's murderer, death reigns over all generations of men without exception and sin spreads farther and farther abroad.

The latest written sections of the Law faithfully preserve this outlook: "If you live by my law, if you remember my commands and obey them, rain shall fall on you when fall it should; the land will yield its increase, and the trees will be bowed with fruit, threshing not done with by vintage time, or vintage by seed-time; you shall have food to your heart's content. Securely you shall hold your lands; sleep safe in your beds, with peace on all your frontiers" (Lev. 26. 3–5).

When the wise men of Israel, giving their spiritual experience in condensed form as maxims, utter their earliest teaching, they repeat the same truth without wearying. We read as follows in the Proverbs, the collection of which began in the time of Solomon: "Son and grandson shall be the good man's heirs; the sinner lays up wealth for nobler men" (Prov. 13. 22). "The just man's home guards its treasure well; the hopes of the wicked are all confusion" (Prov. 15. 6).

The Psalms too, which form Israel's poetical response to revelation, return to this idea often; but not quite so often, for new problems have arisen. The whole of the first psalm, which is a sort of preface to the psalter, is built on this theme:

Blessed is the man who does not guide his steps by ill counsel,
    Or linger where sinners walk,
    Or, where corrupt souls gather, sit down to rest;
The man whose heart is set on the law of the Lord,

On that law, day and night, his thoughts still dwell.
He stands firm as a tree planted by running water,
    Ready to yield its fruit when the season comes,
    And never shedding its leaf;
        All that he does will prosper.
Not such, not such the wicked;
The wicked are like dust, swept away by a wind from the face
    of the earth.
    Not for the wicked, when judgment comes,
    To rise up and plead their cause;
Sinners will have no part in the reunion of the just.
They walk, the just, under the eye of the Lord's favour;
    The path of the wicked, how soon it is lost to sight!

This teaching of the two ways became immensely popular. It is to be found in the writings of the Qumran sect, in the letter of Pseudo-Barnabas and other Christian writings. It remains valid in spite of the many apparent and noticeable exceptions. The same message appears in Psalm 90, sung at Sunday Compline: "He who lives under the protection of the most High, under his heavenly care content to abide, can say to the Lord, Thou art my support and my stronghold, my God, in whom I trust."

Nothing can trouble the man whom God covers with his wings. Again, among many others, may be quoted Psalm 111, the *Beatus vir* of Sunday Vespers. There is no better expression of the thought that all goes well for the devout man who finds his pleasure in the will of God: "Esteem dwells with such a man, and great prosperity; fame shall ever record his bounty. Patient his heart remains and steadfast, quietly he waits for the downfall of his enemies" (Psalm 111. 3, 7).

No doubt exceptions had already been noticed to the general rule that the good are happy, the wicked punished. If it were always observed we should have too simplified a world where there would be no merit in faith or hope. But an answer to the difficulty readily occurred, which prevented the problem from being felt immediately in all it sharpness. The Israelites, like all orientals, have a deep-rooted sense of the clan, the family. The wives and children of Core, Dathan and Abiron were clearly not all to blame for the revolt of these leaders against Moses. Nevertheless, no one was surprised to see the earth open and swallow them all up together. Collective responsibility appeared the natural thing. This or that sinner continued to enjoy the blessing merited by his fathers. Thus Solomon escaped rejection for the sake of David. This or that good man continued to be punished for the wrongdoing of his ancestors. "We have sinned with our fathers." It was all so simple that it was a long time before anyone questioned it.

The great prophets, however, and above all Jeremias and Ezechiel, did not hesitate to state the problem. Without wishing to question the truth already established they brought out clearly the distinction between the lot of the individual and that of the nation. It is given by Jeremias as a feature of the Messianic age: "When that time comes, no more shall be heard of the proverb, The fathers have eaten sour grapes, and the children's teeth are being set on edge; tooth of eater shall ache now, and a man's own guilt shall be a man's own doom" (Jer. 31. 29–30).

For Ezechiel the moral responsibility of each individual applies from the present time onwards: "His father, a man of wrong and violence, that deserved ill of his countrymen, has paid for his guilt by death; would you have the son, too, make amends for it? Nay, but here is a man upright and honest, that holds fast by decrees of mine and obeys them; he must live on. It is the guilty soul that must die; not for the son the father's punishment, not for the father the son's; good shall befall the good, evil the evil" (Ezech. 18. 18–20).

To us, who have been influenced by nineteenth-century individualism, words like these almost seem truisms. There is greater need for us to be recalled to a social sense, to be made to realize that there exists a certain solidarity between man and man. But in the environment of the kingdom of Juda in the years of its decline, and in that of the exile, there was need to proclaim that each by his loyalty or disloyalty towards God brought happiness or misfortune on himself. This new realization, combined with the sufferings of the exile and the development of the "Wisdom" tradition, soon led to the posing of this question: how did it come about that certain national misfortunes did not correspond to the real culpability of the people?

Psalm 43, which dates possibly from the Persian, possibly from the Machabean period, gives forceful expression to this feeling:

> Thou hast disowned us, and put us to shame,
> By refusing to go into battle with our armies.
> Thou dost put us to flight before our enemies;
> Our ill-wishers plunder us as they will.
> Thou hast made us like sheep sold for food,
> Scattered here and there among the heathen;
> Thou hast bartered thy people away without profit,
> Asking no rich amends for thy loss.
> All this has come upon us,
> And it was not that we had forgotten thee.
> We have not been untrue to thy covenant,
> Or withdrawn our hearts from thee,
> That thou shouldst let our steps wander away from thy paths.
> Why hast thou brought us so low,
> With misery all around us,
> And the shadow of death hanging over us?
> If we had forgotten the name of our own God,
> And spread out our hands in prayer to the gods of the alien,
> Would not he know of it?
> He can read the secrets of men's hearts.

(Ps. 43. 10–13, 18–22).

It is a difficult problem. But there follows another of no less magnitude: there exist deliberately impious and sinful people who appear to enjoy happiness on earth. The whole of Psalm 72 is devoted to this puzzle of the prosperity of the wicked:

> Yet I came near to losing my foothold,
> Felt the ground sink under my steps,
> So indignant was I at seeing the good fortune
> Of sinners that defy his law.
> Not for these to share man's common lot of trouble;
> The plagues which afflict humankind still pass them by.
> No wonder if they are overcome with pride,
> Flaunt their lawlessness and impiety.
> How malice distils from those pampered lives;
> How easily they attain the desire of their hearts!
>
> (Ps. 72. 2–3, 5–7)

There is here a terrible stumbling-block. The psalmist gives a preliminary explanation for his own satisfaction: this prosperity of the wicked cannot last for very long. "The truth is, thou dost repay their treacheries, thou, at the height of their fortune, dost overthrow them; what a ruin is theirs!" (Psalm 72. 18).

The righteous, on the other hand, possess God. What more could they want? "What else does heaven hold for me, but thyself? What pleasure should I find in all thy gifts on earth? This frame, this earthly being of mine must come to an end; still God will comfort my heart, God will be, eternally, my inheritance" (Psalm 72. 25–6).

This is a magnificent answer. Has it solved the riddle? At least it leads the writer to the ascetic life and pure love. But it ignores the punishment of the sinner in the next life. And is it understood what form communion with God will take after death? Clearly, revelation was taking a step forward, but darkness was still mingled with the supernatural brightness, and it was necessary still to wait for further illumination.

By contrast good people could be seen who had appalling sufferings. A good third of the Psalms are psalms of complaint and sorrow. While some are songs of repentance where the psalmist is well aware that he suffers for his sins, there are others whose author has no memory of having deserved such punishment. There is the case of the psalm we have just left: "Why then, thought I, it is to no purpose that I have kept my heart true, and washed my hands clean among pure souls" (Psalm 72. 13).

The last prophets, those after the captivity, find themselves forced to deal with this subject: "Complain you did: who serves God serves him for nothing; what reward is ours for keeping command of his, attending with sad mien the Lord of hosts? Here are proud folk more to be envied than we" (Malachias 3. 14–15).

It is to this question that the books of Job and Tobias are especially devoted.

The story of Job, a good man who did not belong to the Jewish people, is well known: how the Adversary was jealous of him; how he experienced terrible afflictions in his possessions and his family, then in his own body through a frightful disease; how despite his sufferings he refused to blaspheme the name of God, and was at last rewarded by the rapid recovery of health and fortune. He is no doubt a historical figure. The prophet Ezechiel speaks of him as a person who might plead on behalf of Israel (Ezechiel 14. 14). This, how-ever, is of little importance. The book of Job is a "wisdom" poem, introduced by a lofty passage where we are taken into the innermost council-chamber of God. There follows a series of discourses attributed to Job's friends, the wise men, Eli-phaz the Themanite, Baldad the Suhite, and Sophar the Naamathite. Further on occurs the enigmatic figure of Eliu. All, on the strength of their honest, but somewhat narrow, "wisdom", maintain that it is impossible that Job should be subjected to such misfortune without his having incurred it

by his sins. To each discourse Job replies patiently by assert-
ing his innocence. At the end of the poem God himself intervenes and replies to Job, before the brief epilogue telling
how the hero of this suffering was rewarded for his patience
and loyalty.

We need not reject everything in the traditional thesis
defended by Job's friends. The first speaker, Eliphaz, is a wise
man, venerable for his learning and tried experience. His
speech is friendly, persuasive, careful not to offend the man
he is addressing. He would like to win him over, to convert
him:

> Speak we, it may be thou wilt take our words amiss,
> Yet speech will out.
> And, sure enough, ruin never fell yet on the innocent;
> Never yet was an upright soul lost to memory.
> The men that traffic in wrong-doing,
> That sow a crop of mischief
> They themselves must reap at last,
> These I have seen undone;
> One breath, one blast of the divine anger
> Withers them quite, and they are gone.
> Can man have right on his side,
> The voice then asked, when he is matched with God?
> Can a mortal creature shew blameless
> In its Creator's presence?
> Happy the man, whom God chastens for his faults!
> The correction he sends thee never, on thy life, refuse.
> Wounds he, it is but to heal;
> The same hand, which smote, shall medicine thee.

(Job 4. 2, 7–9, 17; 5. 17–18)

Baldad is hasty—younger, no doubt. He ignores the degree
of the complexity of life:

> What, still at thy old complaining;
> Blustering still, like a high wind, in vain?
> Can sentence undeserved come from God,
> Unjust award from the Almighty?

What if these children of thine committed some fault,
And he allowed justice to take its course?
For thyself, thou hast but to keep early tryst with God . . .
He will give thee audience betimes.
Ask counsel of the ages that are long past;
Let the experience of former men overrule thee.

(Job 8. 2–6, 8)

Sophar, intervening in his turn, is a fierce character. He does not spare sarcasm:

So ready to speak, be ready in thy turn to listen;
Glibness will not make an innocent man of thee.
Must all keep silence till thou hast done;
Shall none make answer to thy raillery?

(Job 11. 2–3)

This theology has been termed academic. Certainly it is somewhat rough-and-ready. It oversimplifies the order of the world. No Christian would wish to make his own the precise words of Job's lamentation: "This the request that I would make of God, that he would finish what he has begun, crush me altogether, strike a full blow and make an end of me! Consolation enough, if he will but torment me to my death; no repining, then, against his will!" (Job 6. 9–10).

No doubt his great sufferings are an excuse for this. But listen further: "Oh that I had such a pair of scales as might weigh provocation of mine against the ills I suffer! The sand on the shore of ocean could not match the burden of them, and do you wonder that my utterance is all reproach? Deep the Lord's arrows rankle in me, draining my life" (Job 6. 2–4).

Understandably this is found disconcerting by a handful of "wise men" whose life is passed repeating in a thousand different aphorisms the theme that virtue leads to happiness and crime brings with it misfortune. That is the common experience, and the contrary facts are only an exception. True, it is this exception which it is our task to explain.

Then another person comes on the scene, intervening without any warning. This is Eliu. He is young, but his argument is succinct. We may wonder whether his discourse is not an addition to the original work made by a "wise man", unsatisfied both by the attacks of Job's friends and the afflicted man's replies. Job does wrong to blame God, who cannot do anything unjust. His trials are graces sent to train and teach him: "This is one means by which he will turn a man away from his designs, purge him of his pride; and so the grave is disappointed, the sword misses its prey. Or else he will use the pains of the sick-bed for a man's correction, and leave his whole frame wasted with disease" (Job 33. 17–19).

Next comes the theophany. God himself manifests his wisdom and power to Job in superb language and wonderful poetry. He shows him that he cannot dispute with God. "From what vantage-point wast thou watching, when I laid the foundations of the earth? Tell me, whence comes this sure knowledge of thine? Tell me, since thou art so wise, was it thou or I designed earth's plan, measuring it out with the line?" (Job 38. 4–5).

It may thus be said that without giving the problem of evil a clear-cut and definitive solution the book of Job offers us three compatible but incomplete solutions. Revelation is not finished—far from it. But all three solutions are, nevertheless, illuminating and worth our meditation. The first appears in the speech of God, which is the climax of the work. It is a call to trust in the infinite wisdom of God. Human wisdom cannot judge God. It must accept what it does not understand. Confidence in the goodness of him, who provides the raven with his food: "Which of us feeds the ravens? Is it not to God their nestlings cry so shrilly, homeless for want of food?" (Job 38. 41), if it explains nothing, is at least the most comforting and simple attitude. The second solution, already indicated in the prologue and partly taken up by Job's friends, is set in relief by the speeches of Eliu. Suffering is a trial by which God makes sure of the loyalty of his own, as well as a spiritual training which gives the soul maturity and strength. "It is the friendless he rescues ... speaks home to them through the afflictions they endure" (Job 36. 15; *cf.* 33. 17–19 *cit. sup.*).

The third solution is the jealousy of the devil, indicated also in the prologue. It is implied in the third chapter of Genesis and is taken up by St John.

On a first reading a fourth solution seems to be hinted at, namely, retribution in the next world. The Vulgate places on Job's lips these splendid words: "For I know that my Redeemer liveth, and in the last day I shall rise out of the earth. And I shall be clothed again with my skin: and in my flesh I shall see my God" (Job 19. 25–26: Douai Version). This text, used in a responsory of the Office of the Dead, is a clear expression of Christian belief. But the Greek Septuagint Version is less clear: "For I know that he who is to deliver me, to raise up my skin, that endures these things, upon the earth, is eternal; for it is the Lord who has accomplished this for me." As for the original, it is still less clear on the subject of survival. "But I know that my redeemer liveth, and that he shall stand up at the last upon the earth: and after my skin has been thus destroyed, yet from my flesh shall I see God" (Revised Version).

The recompense of a glorious, resurrected body still seems very obscure to the primitive poet. Gradually revelation becomes more defined and brings increasing consolation to the afflicted soul.[1]

The book of Tobias repeats much the same teaching, with less grandeur and poetry, but in a more human and touching

---

[1] The book of Ecclesiastes does not deal with the problem of evil directly but it demonstrates the incomplete character of earthly goods. All the sources of human happiness are incapable of providing satisfaction. Everywhere we meet vanity and deception, because God has set eternity in man's heart (Eccles. 3. 11).

manner. We see a devout Israelite family afflicted to an exceptional degree, first by exile in Assyria after the fall of Samaria, then by persecution of which the Jews, with their particularism and somewhat aggressive tendencies, have everywhere been the object, and finally by Tobias' blindness. Tobias' poverty is such that his wife has to go out to work to help her young son earn the family's daily bread.

Next we meet a young girl called Sara, also strangely unfortunate, in spite of her youth and beauty, because of the sad fate of her successive suitors. For the writer of the book misfortune is a trial in the full sense, turned by God's providence to the advantage of those who endure it with faith. There is great insistence on the rôle of angels. It is the evil spirit Asmodaeus who persecutes Sara and kills her suitors one after the other. It is the angel Raphael (a name meaning "God heals") who brings to God the prayers and almsgiving of Tobias, accompanies his son on his journey, marries him to Sara after delivering her from Asmodaeus, brings the son back with joy to his father, and finally sets the old man free from his infirmity. The field of battle between the angels and the evil spirits, which we catch sight of clearly in the Gospels, is evoked here, but on a modest scale, in the destinies of a single family.

If the book of Tobias is not in its entirety a pious fiction —though there is nothing to prevent this literary form being honoured by the charisma of inspiration—we are unable to determine what part of its contents is history properly so called. In the books of Machabees we encounter history in the full sense, at a particularly unhappy period. It is the moment of the terrible persecution of Antiochus Epiphanes and the first martyrs. Here the problem of suffering becomes clearer: the punishment of the wicked, the persecutors, the blasphemers, is heavy in proportion to the blame their wrongdoing deserves: "So died he [Antiochus], wretchedly enough, the murderer, the blasphemer, out in the hill country far away from home. Cruel the blow that struck him down, as he had ever been cruel in his dealings" (2 Mach. 9. 28).

The trials endured by the chosen people are a correction inflicted on them by God by means of their enemies, who are unconscious instruments of divine justice. The sixth of the seven Machabean brothers cries to the tyrant who is having him tortured: "Never flatter thyself with vain hope; speed we amiss, it was our own doing, that sinned against our God" (2 Mach. 7. 18).

The sufferings of the martyrs are a means of reconciliation. Moreover, from now on there is clear mention of the future life and its rewards, out of proportion to the torments endured. "Brief pains, that under his warrant have seized my brethren of eternal life! And shalt not thou, by his sentence, pay the deserved penalty of thy pride?" (2 Mach. 7. 36).

The glorious prospect of the resurrection of the body is now unfolded before the eyes of the martyrs and gives them powerful encouragement: "Of this present life it lies in thy power to rob us, but he, who is ruler of the whole world, he, for whose laws we perish, will raise us up again, and to life everlasting" (2 Mach. 7. 9).

It is, however, important to notice that revelation is not only made through the inspired writings but through ordinary religious teaching, traces of which we find scattered through numerous apocryphal works. The Sadducees never accepted this doctrine of the resurrection. Possibly they thought it a greater perfection to work for God without the hope of an eternal reward. On this point the Pharisees were more sensitive to the word of God. Their teaching spread among the souls that were most devout, most generous, most open to the light.

It is in the book of Wisdom, written at Alexandria more than fifty years before the birth of Christ, that the Old Testament revelation attains the greatest degree of clarity on the subject of evil and suffering, by demonstrating clearly the immortality of the soul and, in consequence, the reality of retribution in the next world. What in fact made the weight of suffering difficult to bear was the impression of the people of Israel that all must be settled in this life: "From the dead, Lord, thou hast no praises, the men who go down into the place of silence" (Ps. 113. 25). Or again: "Give me some respite, some cool breath of comfort, before I go away and am known no more" (Ps. 38. 14).

Only the faint after-life of Sheol was recognized, where souls, far from God, lead the most shadowy existence. Doubtless it was increasingly felt that divine justice required that on the other side of the grave the injustices of this life should be set right. Time and again the psalmists express the hope, perhaps the assurance, that they will never know separation from God: "Thou wilt not leave my soul in the place of death, or allow thy faithful servant to see corruption. Thou hast shewn me the way of life; thou wilt make me full of gladness in thy presence; at thy right hand are delights that will endure for ever" (Ps. 15. 10–11).

And later: "But my life God will rescue from the power of that lower darkness, a life that finds acceptance with him" (Ps. 48. 16).

Belief in the resurrection of the body had been affirmed continually in the books of Machabees, as we have seen. In the book of Wisdom the Jewish faith emerges from having been in contact with Greek thought. This helped to free it from the old imprecise and undefined idea represented for the Hebrews by "the breath of life". By gaining a clearer idea of the soul, Israel realized in God's light that the soul is immortal: "Death was never of God's fashioning: not for his pleasure does life cease to be" (Wisdom 1. 13).

Henceforth, without losing all its mystery, the question of evil is solved in a way that can bring consolation:

> But the souls of the just are in God's hands,
> And no torment, in death itself, has power to reach them.

Dead? Fools think so; think their end loss,
Their leaving us annihilation; but all is well with them.
The world sees nothing but the pains they endure;
They themselves have eyes only for what is immortal;
So light their suffering, so great the gain they win!
God, all the while, did but test them,
And testing them found them worthy of him.
His gold, tried in the crucible,
His burnt sacrifice, graciously accepted,
They do but wait for the time of their deliverance.

(Wisdom 3. 1–6)

Similarly, the impious and the wicked receive the penalty
their life has earned:

Far, it seems, did our thoughts wander from the true path;
Never did the ray of justice enlighten them,
Never the true sun shone.
Weary it proved, the reckless way of ruin,
Lonely the wastes we travelled,
Who missed the path the Lord meant for us.
What advantage has it brought us, all our pomp and pride?
How are we better for all our vaunted wealth?

(Wisdom 5. 6–8)

Henceforth it will be realized that Wisdom is the most
precious of good things. It always ends by bringing happiness;
human setbacks are only apparent, it is eternal life which is
really important. As for the redemptive character of suffering,
glimpses of it occur here and there, within very narrow limits,
it must be owned. Thus Moses offers God to give his life to
save the people. "Thy people have sinned heinously, in making themselves gods of gold. I entreat thee, pardon this offence
of theirs; or else blot out my name too from the record thou
hast written" (Exod. 32. 31–32).

Likewise, the Lord's servant in Deutero-Isaias is praised
for having made his life a sacrifice for sin: "And all the while
it was for our sins he was wounded, it was guilt of ours

crushed him down; on him the punishment fell that brought us peace, by his bruises we were healed. His life laid down for guilt's atoning, he shall yet be rewarded; father of a long posterity, instrument of the divine purpose; for all his heart's anguish, rewarded in full" (Isaias 53. 5, 10, 11).

It seems as though revelation is complete. The causes of suffering, the way of subduing it in practice and the bright prospect which its recompense affords are known from now on, but it remains true that God, in his infinite peace, seems to be ignorant of what suffering means. He makes it the lot of his friends, of those, sometimes, whom he has privileged. Even an untimely death could be a mark of favour on the part of God: "Divine favour, divine love banished him from a life he shared with sinners, caught him away, before wickedness could pervert his thoughts, before wrong-doing could allure his heart; ... with him early achievement counted for long apprenticeship" (Wisdom 4. 10–11, 13).

Yet, in the Old Testament the Poet's resigned complaint would have been well understood: "I know that you have other things to do than to pity us all, and that a child who dies, bringing despair to his mother, makes no difference to you. I know that the fruit falls at the shaking of the wind, that the bird loses its plumage and the flower its scent; that Creation is an immense wheel which cannot move without crushing someone."[2] But God himself will know suffering by human experience.

[2] Victor Hugo, *Les Contemplations.*

CHAPTER V

THE NEW TESTAMENT

The Incarnation gave the Son of God the power to suffer in exactly the same way as men. The epistle to the Hebrews sets this in striking relief: "God is the last end of all things, the first beginning of all things; and it befitted his majesty that, in summoning all those sons of his to glory, he should crown with suffering the life of that Prince who was to lead them into salvation" (Hebrews 2. 10).

This was due to the priesthood he was to exercise: "Christ, during his earthly life, offered prayer and entreaty to God who could save him from death, not without a piercing cry, not without tears; yet with such piety as won him a hearing. Son of God though he was, he learned obedience in the school of suffering, and now, his full achievement reached, he wins eternal salvation for all those who render obedience to him" (Hebrews 5. 7–9).

And he preserves throughout eternity with his human nature the experience he has gained of our wretchedness: "It is not as if our high priest was incapable of feeling for us in our humiliations; he has been through every trial, fashioned as we are, only sinless" (Hebrews 4. 15).

In the Gospel the problem is not evaded. This is the first thing we notice and it is of the greatest value to us. Evil appears as evil, and not only moral, but also physical evil. Christ is not afraid to talk of hell as the consequence of sin: "If thy right eye is the occasion of thy falling into sin, pluck

it out and cast it away from thee; better to lose one part of
thy body than to have the whole cast into hell" (Matt. 5. 29).
Or again: "And there is no need to fear those who kill thy
body, but have no means of killing the soul; fear him more,
who has the power to ruin body and soul in hell" (Matt.
10. 28).

This is the supreme, the irreparable, evil. But suffering is
also an evil, and Jesus does not hesitate to show fear at the
approach of his passion. On Palm Sunday, after the declara-
tion that his hour has come, and that the grain of wheat yields
no fruit unless it passes through death, he cries: "And now
my soul is distressed. What am I to say? I will say, Father,
save me from undergoing this hour of trial; and yet, I have
only reached this hour of trial that I might undergo it" (John
12. 27).

And when the moment of suffering arrives, when he goes
to the Garden of Gethsemane where the traitor is to come and
seize him, he does not hide his sorrow, aversion and fear.
"Father, if it pleases thee, take away this chalice from before
me . . ." He accepts the encouragement the angel brings him.
In his agony he prays with greater earnestness: "His sweat
fell to the ground like thick drops of blood" (Luke 22. 42, 44).

Rather astonishingly several manuscripts of St Luke omit
this passage. The ideal the Stoics had given the world was a
wisdom, a severity, which tried to ignore suffering. In the
pagan world, which St Paul takes to task for its heartlessness,
it is strength which attracts admiration. Those who have no
strength pretend to have it. It was a sort of inheritance from
the Spartan austerity. But although many of the martyrs have
gone to torture and death without letting their suffering be
seen for joy at meeting Christ, Jesus himself, the king of
martyrs, wished to suffer more simply. He did not deny his
pain, but accepted it and offered it for the salvation of the
world: "Take away this chalice from me; only as thy will is,
not as mine is" (Mark 14. 36).

With the same simplicity Christ feels deeply the suffering of others. At the gate of Naim he meets the funeral procession of a young man, the only son of a widow. Seeing the poor mother he was moved with compassion for her (Luke 7. 13). And this pity made him work one of his greatest miracles. Nor did the physical needs of the people leave him unmoved. We hear him exclaim: "I am moved with pity for the multitude; it is three days now since they have been in attendance on me, and they have nothing to eat. If I send them back to their homes fasting, they will grow faint on their journey" (Mark 8. 2–3).

Still less does he forget spiritual hunger: "Jesus saw a great multitude there, and took pity on them, since they were like sheep that have no shepherd, and began to give them long instruction" (Mark 6. 34).

He is to be seen full of commiseration for his friend Lazarus and his sisters Martha and Mary in their grief: "So Mary reached the place where Jesus was; and when she saw him, she fell at his feet; Lord, she said, if thou hadst been here, my brother would not have died. And Jesus, when he saw her in tears, and the tears of the Jews who accompanied her, sighed deeply, and distressed himself over it; Where have you buried him? he asked. Lord, they said to him, come and see. Then Jesus wept. See, said the Jews, how he loved him" (John 11. 32–6). Lines like this need no comment. Here one sees clearly that Jesus plays no tricks with evil. He shares simply in the suffering men endure.

Some days later, at the time of his triumphal entry as Messias on Palm Sunday, seeing from the Mount of Olives Jerusalem below him in all its splendour, the thought seizes our Lord of the terrible siege which is going to lay it low. Then, too, he is moved to tears: "And as he drew near, and caught sight of the city, he wept over it, and said: Ah, if thou too couldst understand, above all in this day that is granted thee, the ways that can bring thee peace! As it is, they are

hidden from thy sight. The days will come upon thee when
thy enemies will fence thee round about, and encircle thee,
and press thee hard on every side, and bring down in ruin
both thee and thy children that are in thee, not leaving one
stone of thee upon another; and all because thou didst not
recognize the time of my visiting thee" (Luke 19. 41–5).

The words spoken by our Lord to the daughters of Jerusalem who followed him on the road to Calvary betray
exactly the same concern (Luke 23. 27–31). St Matthew can
make the saying of Isaias apply to him to the letter: "He took
our infirmities upon himself, and bore our sickness" (Matt.
8. 17). There was no human suffering which he had not
known and made his own by this personal experience. It is
this which has made him the perfect head of the restored
human race.

While bringing alleviation to the sick, Christ gave various
instructions on the origin of evil. An illness can be the punishment of sin. When in the temple he meets the paralytic healed
by him at the pool of Bethsaida, he says to him: "Behold,
thou hast recovered thy strength; do not sin any more, for
fear that worse should befall thee" (John 5. 14). Sometimes
he emphasizes the devil's malice: "And here is this daughter
of Abraham, whom Satan had kept bound these eighteen years
past; was it wrong that she should be delivered on the sabbath
day from bonds like these?" (Luke 13. 16).

Elsewhere he makes it clear that physical evil is not necessarily the punishment of a personal sin: "Master, was this
man guilty of sin, or was it his parents, that he should have
been born blind? Neither he nor his parents were guilty, Jesus
answered; it was so that God's action might declare itself in
him" (John 9. 2–3). In another context, concerning a disaster
which had plunged the poorer quarter of Jerusalem in mourning: "What of those eighteen men on whom the tower fell in
Siloe, and killed them; do you suppose that there was a

heavier account against them, than against any others who
then dwelt at Jerusalem?" (Luke 13. 4). What we are told in
all this is somewhat vague. None of these sayings envisages
more than a particular case and all reveal chiefly Christ's
knowledge of men's hearts: "He did not need assurances about
any man, because he could read men's hearts" (John 2. 25).

On the other hand the *lumen gloriae*[1] which Christ enjoyed
gave him a perfect serenity. For him sin and suffering were
sad facts, but he did not experience the stumbling-block their
existence constitutes for us. Even evil enters into the plan of
the kingdom of God. The kingdom, as it is here on earth,
comprises not only the good seed which is the word of God,
but also the tares: these are the children of the evil one, the
enemy who has sown them is the devil. It would be an oversimplification to divide the world into good and bad people.
The truth is that the wicked are not completely wicked, but
preserve their good sides, that the good are not entirely irre-
proachable, but retain their evil inclinations, and that all are
sinners. As the most profound interpreter of our Lord's
thought put it, "Sin is with us; if we deny that, we are cheating
ourselves; it means that truth does not dwell in us" (1 John
1. 8). That is the reason why the roots of the wheat are in-
extricably mixed with those of the tares. For the moment the
weed cannot be rooted up without at the same time damaging
the corn: "The tares were gathered together and burned in the
fire, and so it will be when the world is brought to an end; the
Son of Man will give charge to his angels, and they will gather
up all that gives offence in his kingdom, all those who do
wickedly in it" (Matt. 13. 40–1).

And amazingly, by a paradox which bears witness to the
power of the divine plan, suffering becomes the normal way
to glory. The disciples, even the apostles, have great difficulty
in entering into this thought. When our Lord speaks for the

[1] "Light of glory", that is, the light in which his human mind saw
the beatific vision. (*Trans.*)

first time of his cross, St Peter, although he has just pro-
claimed him the Messias, the Son of the living God, thinks
himself entitled to reprove his Master: "Never, Lord, he said;
no such thing shall befall thee." He is taken aback to hear
our Lord answer him with great vehemence: "Back, Satan;
thou art a stone in my path; for these thoughts of thine are
man's, not God's" (Matt. 16. 22–3). And though our Lord
repeated this prophecy on many occasions, it was only a
waste of time: "They could make nothing of all this; his
meaning was hidden from them, so that they could not understand what he said" (Luke 18. 34).

It is no small surprise to us that it should be one of the
thieves crucified with our Lord who seems to have been the
first to discover the road which leads to glory by way of
the cross. "Lord," he said, "remember me when thou comest
into thy kingdom" (Luke 23. 42).

No Jew, in thinking of the Messias, had ever placed side
by side the prophecies of glory and those of suffering and
humiliation. And when our Lord appeared to the two disciples
on the road to Emmaus he had to open their eyes for them
to see something of the mystery: "Was it not to be expected
that the Christ should undergo these sufferings, and enter so
into his glory?" (Luke 24. 26).

Again it takes a long discourse to show them by means of
Scripture that all this was willed by God and foreseen by
him. Just as our Lord accepts suffering as his own lot, so he
accepts it for all those who belong to him. For his mother:
"as for thy own soul, it shall have a sword to pierce it" (Luke
2. 35).

Similarly he accepts it for his disciples:

> If any man has a mind to come my way, let him renounce
> self, and take up his cross, and follow me. The man who tries
> to save his life shall lose it; it is the man who loses his life
> for my sake that will secure it. (Matt. 16. 24–5.)

Believe me when I tell you this, you will weep and lament while the world rejoices; you will be distressed, but your distress shall be turned into joy. A woman in childbirth feels distress, because now her time has come; but when she has borne her child, she does not remember the distress any longer, so glad is she that a man has been born into the world. So it is with you, you are distressed now; but one day I will see you again, and then your hearts will be glad. (John 16. 20–2.)

Words like these are often on his lips: "Do not forget what I said to you, No servant can be greater than his master. They will persecute you just as they have persecuted me" (John 15. 20). "In the world, you will only find tribulation; but take courage, I have overcome the world" (John 16. 33).

But there is an extraordinary reversal of values, for our Lord affirms, and spiritual experience proves, that suffering does not prevent happiness, but actually, in its own way, contributes to happiness. This is the doctrine of the beatitudes. The poor, the patient, those who weep, those who hunger for holiness, those who suffer persecution, are those who know suffering. Nevertheless, happiness is theirs. Manifestly, it is not complete on earth. It will only be really perfect in heaven; but it begins here below. Already the poor receive the kingdom as their share, the patient inherit the land, the clean of heart begin to have a glimpse of God: "Blessed are you, when men revile you, and persecute you, and speak all manner of evil against you falsely, because of me. Be glad and light-hearted" (Matt. 5. 11–12).

In Jesus Christ the future is present. "The promised happiness is not a hypothetical consolation prize, it is the word of him who can see and judge the present from the point of view of the last hour".[2] It is those who suffer who are the privileged beneficiaries of the Gospel. The others, the rich, the contented, have no room left for God. They are satisfied with their lot and have no aspirations after a destiny, a happi-

[2] M. Bouttier, *Vocabulaire biblique*, p. 121.

ness, which passes their comprehension. They neither love, nor seek, "the things that are above" (Coloss. 3. 1).

That is the meaning of the curses which are attached to the beatitudes: "But woe upon you who are rich. . . . Woe upon you who are filled full. . . . Woe upon you who laugh now. . . . Woe upon you, when all men speak well of you" (Luke 6. 24–6).

The central point of New Testament teaching on the subject of evil is obviously the redemption of the world by the suffering and death of Christ. Gradually increasing light is thrown on this point. When Joseph, worried because of Mary's pregnancy, hesitates about taking her as his wife, reassuring him the angel says: "*And she will bear a son, whom thou shalt call Jesus* (which means Saviour), *for he is to save his people*, not from the Roman domination nor from the hardships inherent in the human condition, but *from their sins*" (Matt. 1. 21).

This salvation is to come not only from his ethical preaching turning men away from evil, nor from the force of his example, but from his sufferings and his death. It is a curious fact that the word "redemption" is much less frequent in the New Testament than in the Old, but it is the only word that can show precisely the meaning of our Lord's death: "The Son of Man came to give his life as a *ransom* for the lives of many" (Mark 10. 45).

Numerous passages from the writings of the apostles provide, as it were, an orchestration for the theme of this utterance of Christ: "A great price was paid to *ransom* you; glorify God by making your bodies the shrines of his presence" (1 Cor. 6. 20). And further on: "A price was paid to *redeem* you; do not enslave yourselves to human masters" (1 Cor. 7. 23).

To his disciple Timothy St Paul writes: "There is only one God, and only one mediator between God and men, Jesus

Christ, who is a man, like them, and gave himself as a *ransom* for them all" (1 Tim. 2. 5–6). And to Titus: "Our Saviour Jesus Christ; who gave himself for us, to *ransom* us from all our guilt, a people set apart for himself" (Titus 2. 13–14).

The author of the epistle to the Hebrews shows us Jesus Christ entering right into the Holy of Holies, that is, into the intimacy of the Deity, bringing, not the blood of goats and calves, like the Jewish high-priest, but his own blood, and winning thereby a *ransom* that lasts for ever (Hebrews 9. 12).

St Peter, addressing the newly baptized, asks them: "What was the *ransom* that freed you from the vain observances of ancestral tradition? You know well enough that it was not paid in earthly currency, silver or gold; it was paid in the precious blood of Christ; no lamb was ever so pure, so spotless a victim" (1 Peter 1. 18–19).

In the Apocalypse of St John we see all heaven prostrate before the Lamb singing this hymn: "Thou, Lord, art worthy to take up the book and break the seals that are on it. Thou wast slain in sacrifice, out of every tribe, every language, every people, every nation thou hast *ransomed* us with thy blood and given us to God" (Apoc. 5. 9).

St John had given the same teaching at the beginning of his gospel reporting the words of John the Baptist: "Look, this is the Lamb of God; look, this is he who takes away the sin of the world" (John 1. 29).

The fact that the sin of the world called for so much suffering throws a strong light on the nature of moral evil. It is not without reason that all four evangelists, so sparing in their treatment of the life of our Lord as a whole, give such circumstantial details of his passion. The impression is given that the apostolic college insisted on our Lord's crucifixion being *pictured* (cf. Gal. 3. 1) as vividly as possible, in spite of the scandal this could cause. Note, too, that there reappears in St John, albeit transfigured, the old myth of the conflict of light and darkness: "When the light came into the world men preferred darkness to light; preferred it, because their doings were evil ... the man whose life is true comes to the light" (John 3. 19–21). The light is Christ himself: "I am the light of the world, he said. He who follows me can never walk in darkness" (John 8. 12).

The darkness is the spiritual disposition of wicked souls. Our Lord says this plainly to the Jews: "Why is it that you cannot understand the language I talk? It is because you have no ear for the message I bring. You belong to your father, that is, the devil, and are eager to gratify the appetites which are your father's. He, from the first, was a murderer; and as for truth, he has never taken his stand upon that; there is no truth in him" (John 8. 43–4).

The Prince of darkness, the Prince of this world, has an ascendancy over them (*cf.* John 14. 30). When the light pre-vails it is faith putting into effect God's acceptance of men and personal gift to men. When it is darkness that gains the upper hand, it is sin installing itself. But the victory has been won by Christ. The hour of his death ushers in his glorifica-tion and the great increase of the number of his faithful.

On the mystery as a whole the teaching of the apostles could not be more than an echo of that of their Master. How-ever, it does give us further enlightenment on the subject of evil and of suffering in particular. First, St Paul insists that the cross borne by Christians continues and completes the cross of Christ. He writes to the Christians at Colossae: "I am glad of my sufferings on your behalf, as, in this mortal frame of mine, I help to pay off the debt which the afflictions of Christ leave still to be paid, for the sake of his body, the Church" (Coloss. 1. 24).

Obviously, he did not imagine that the sufferings of Christ were insufficient, but he rejoiced and felt honoured to be able to share in the redemption of the world, for it is Christ who continues to suffer in us. Moreover, it is the fact of our belong-

ing to Christ which wins us the most effective suffering: "And
indeed, all those who are resolved to live a holy life in Christ
Jesus will meet with persecution" (2 Tim. 3. 12). All the same,
this only lasts for a time, and will have the most joyful consequences in eternity: "Not that I count these present sufferings as the measure of that glory which is to be revealed in
us" (Romans 8. 18).

St James also emphasizes the eternal reward: "Blessed is
he who endures under trials. When he has proved his worth,
he will win that crown of life, which God has promised to
those who love him" (James 1. 12). Already, here below,
suffering accepted with Christ and for Christ brings its own
joy:

> For ourselves, we are being hampered everywhere, yet still
> have room to breathe, are hard put to it, but never at a loss;
> persecution does not leave us unbefriended, nor crushing blows
> destroy us; we carry about continually in our bodies the dying
> state of Jesus, so that the living power of Jesus may be mani-
> fested in our bodies too.... No, we do not play the coward;
> though the outward part of our nature is being worn down, our
> inner life is refreshed from day to day. This light and momen-
> tary affliction brings with it a reward multiplied every way,
> loading us with everlasting glory. (2 Cor. 4. 8–10, 16–17.)
> [He continues further on:] I am full of encouragement, nay, I
> cannot contain myself for happiness, in the midst of all these
> trials of mine. (2 Cor. 7. 4).

The Apocalypse, written to comfort the Christians in the
first persecutions, provides much encouragement for suffering. Tribulation is at once a warning and a correction. "It is
those I love that I correct and chasten," says our Lord (Apoc.
3. 19). But he himself stays with the persecuted: "I know how
sorely tried thou art, how stricken with poverty (yet, all the
while, so rich): how thy name is traduced by men who claim
to be Jews (though they are no true Jews; they are rather the
chosen people of Satan). Do not be afraid of the suffering
thou art to undergo. Before long, the devil will throw some

of you into prison, to have your faith tested there, and for
ten days you shall be in sore distress. Keep faith with me to
the point of death, and I will crown thee with life" (Apoc.
2. 9–10).

It remains now for us to collect together some points of
apostolic teaching which, though somewhat obscure, nevertheless throw further light on the mystery of evil. First of all
St Paul reveals to us the cosmic character of evil: "If creation
is full of expectancy, that is because it is waiting for the sons
of God to be made known. Created nature has been condemned to frustration; not for some deliberate fault of its
own, but for the sake of him who so condemned it, with a
hope to look forward to; namely, that nature in its turn will
be set free from the tyranny of corruption, to share in the
glorious freedom of God's sons. The whole of nature, as we
know, groans in a common travail all the while" (Romans
8. 19–22).

"Creation" here stands for the totality of material beings,
with the exception of those that are rational. By personifica-
tion the emotions of suspense, hope, impatience, repugnance,
are attributed to it. Viewed as a whole, it groans and suffers
the pains of childbirth. It has, in a manner, been violated,
through the idle and profane uses to which it has been put
since the appearance of sin. It submits, however, to God's
order, but on the twofold assurance that it will one day be
set free and glorified with man. St Paul seems to be making
no allusion here to any sin but man's. Elsewhere he declares
that before Christ's coming creation had been in the devil's
power: "And the dominions and powers he robbed of their
prey, put them to an open shame, led them away in triumph,
through him" (Col. 2. 15).

But in spite of this triumph's having been won and the
victory assured, the struggle continues: "It is not against
flesh and blood (only) that we enter the lists; we have to do

with princedoms and powers, with those who have mastery of the world in these dark days, with malign influence in an order higher than ours" (Ephes. 6. 12).

And so we take our place on an immense battlefield, where the angels and evil spirits have their part to play, Christ having already won the decisive victory. But it is the Apocalypse which evokes in the most forceful manner the diabolic activity running through the age-long struggle constituted by the history of the Church. Here we see first how the origin of evil goes back beyond the rebellion of man, how it took place far earlier, in the revolt of a great band of angels: "Fierce war broke out in heaven, where Michael and his angels fought against the dragon. The dragon and his angels fought on their part, but could not win the day, or stand their ground in heaven any longer; the great dragon, serpent of the primal age, was flung down to earth; he whom we call the devil, or Satan, the whole world's seducer, flung down to earth, and his angels with him" (Apoc. 12. 7–9).

Throughout history, cleverly, we might almost say with consummate art, he has made use of the evil forces that he has liberated in man. Side by side with the dragon is another beast representing Rome of the persecutions, and, more generally, all those political powers which, following the example of ancient Rome, have tried in the course of the centuries to set up their own worship and have persecuted Christians when they refuse to commit this idolatry. The time comes when the persecuting power receives a mortal blow, but it is constantly reborn with its pride and false claims.

Another beast, which John later calls "the false prophet", symbolizes the intellectual forces contributing their influence to the service of the political beast. It succeeds in procuring the worship of the first beast and multiplies the miracles which guarantee its divinity. Finally it stirs up persecution against all who refuse to join in the idolatrous worship of the State. It is the devil, with the help of the forces at his command, who is the cause of the sin, moral suffering and miseries of those who live on the earth. From them too proceed indirectly all the scourges that divine justice uses to punish the guilty. It is Satan again, backed up by his infernal army, who at the end of time will redouble the torments inflicted in like manner on those who refuse to worship the true God. Against him Christ does battle with his faithful. The Seer pictures him, mounted on a white horse, his eyes flashing like flame, clothed in garments stained with blood. His name is the Word of God. The sash which girds him bears the words "the King of kings and the Lord of lords" (cf. Apoc. 19. 12 following). At his side are his faithful putting forth all their efforts. They may be put to death, but scarcely have they crossed the Red Sea of martyrdom before they intone on the other bank the canticle of Moses and the Lamb. Their apparent defeat has in reality been a victory. And the message of Patmos assures us that the struggle will end in the triumph of good, and that Love will remain the victor.

So much we see. It is like a night harassed by violent thunder, and lit up by lightning-flashes, too brief to show us all we want to know. The mystery remains a mystery. St Peter, indeed, tells us that revelation is given to us "like a lamp in some darkened room" (2 Peter 1. 19). A man who goes into a cathedral at night with a flash-lamp cannot properly appreciate the building's architecture. He sees just enough to avoid bumping into the chairs and pillars. So we have enough light to guide our conduct, not enough to appreciate God's work as a whole.

It is well, however, that revelation ends with a description of heaven which, without claiming to give us a complete picture of its grandeur and beauty, sets it before us as the place where God "will wipe away every tear from their eyes, and there will be no more death, or mourning, or cries of distress, no more sorrow; those old things have passed away" (Apoc. 21. 4).

CHAPTER VI

TRADITION

It would be possible to point out a great number of passages from the Fathers where they recall and explain what revelation has to say on the subject of evil: letters of consolation, funeral orations, sermons during public disasters. Here, we confine ourselves to St Augustine and St Thomas not only because they are of prime importance in themselves, but because both have given the fullest treatment to the problem of evil.

Augustine had actually fallen into Manicheism in his student days. The adherents of this sect, whom he calls proud and immoderate, carnal and wordy, had the names of Christ and the Paraclete constantly on their lips. It was like the lime on a snare set by the devil. They repeated incessantly "truth, truth". Nothing could be more attractive to Augustine with all the hunger and thirst of his soul for truth. Unfortunately they could only provide him with a nourishment lacking in reality. On the whole, the delights of poetry, to which the young rhetorician had surrendered himself in the previous years, were worth far more than all the fantasies of the Manicheans. But Augustine remained troubled by the questions they kept on asking: What was the origin of evil? Was God confined to the limits of a bodily form? Had he hair and nails? Must the men of the Old Testament be regarded as saints when they practised polygamy, homicide and animal sacrifice? The young student did not yet know that evil is only the privation of good, privation that ends finally in nothingness. He had no idea of a purely spiritual God nor of true interior justice, which, without changing fundamentally the precepts it gives, does not, however, enforce them at once in all their vigour in an age ill-prepared to receive them. He did not shrink from pouring scorn on God's servants under the old covenant. For nine years—from the age of eighteen to twenty-seven—he remained their dupe. He pursued worldly distinction and literary success, and sought purification from this by taking food and alms to the "elect" of the sect. He himself was only a simple "auditor". He sought for happiness with all his ardent soul, thinking to find it in the beauty of art and literature and in the study of philosophy. But he found no trace of it. Then, when he had just reached the age of twenty-eight, Faustus, a Manichean bishop, a native of Milevis in Numidia, arrived in Carthage. He had an attractive gift of eloquence. Augustine admired the art of fine speaking, but already his philosophical training and the seriousness of his thought enabled him to distinguish truth from unreality, to pay more attention to the food that was served him than to the wonderful dish on which it was presented. He was now in a position to compare the fantasies of Manicheism with the metaphysical reflections of Aristotle which he had just been studying. Doubtless this was not yet knowledge of the living God, but it was enough to make him realize the inadequacy of Manicheism from the scientific point of view. The interminable extravagances of Mani were of far less worth than simpler accounts which nevertheless carried conviction. To make matters worse Mani claimed to be the Holy Ghost in person.

Augustine had never accepted the whole Manichean doctrine, but admitted its essential points: everything is material, including God. Evil is a separate, living substance. The human soul is a part of the deity. Despite his admiration for the skill with which Faustus expressed these ideas, Augustine, finding him always in the middle of a circle of "auditors", longed to submit his difficulties to him in private conversation. At last the opportunity arrived. He discovered from Faustus' conversation that he was wholly without a liberal education, except for grammar, but that he had acquired a real dexterity with words, thanks to his daily exercise in speaking. His incompetence was soon apparent. Augustine had to give up the idea of obtaining any elucidations, as Faustus modestly admitted his inability to provide them. This frankness necessarily engaged his sympathy. So Augustine did not break with the sect, but he despaired already of its ability to satisfy him completely.

This happened just when the young professor was leaving Carthage for Rome, where he had been offered a better post, and where in particular he would find better educated and harder working students than at Carthage. In the capital of the Empire he enjoyed the hospitality of an "auditor" of the sect. Until then he had thought that evil, while existing in us, did not originate with us: "For I still held the view that it was not we who sinned, but that sin was committed in us by some being of a different kind. It pleased my pride thus to avoid being to blame and admitting my responsibility for the wicked things I had done" (*Confessions* V. 10. 18).

He was, however, scandalized by the conduct of certain of the "elect" of the Roman group. Mani's teaching imposed a strict asceticism on the "elect". Not all of them observed it. Soon Augustine set about dissuading his host from trusting too blindly in the writings of Mani and his adepts. For all that he did not break with them. The chief difficulty which held him back was his inability to think of God otherwise than under the aspect of a material mass: "This led me to believe that there was also a substance of evil of similar nature, havings its own foul, hideous form. This might be gross, in which case it was called earth, or thin and transparent like the stuff air is made of. . . . Since what little piety

I had forced me to believe that God in his goodness had not created any naturally evil being, I decided that the two material substances must be opposed to one another, each of them infinite, the good, however, on a more generous, the evil on a more constricted scale. From these pestilential premises the rest of my impieties followed" (*Confessions* V. 10. 20).

This caused a number of difficulties in his view of the Incarnation, for example. Not until he had left Rome for Milan, drawn by the reputation of St Ambrose, did he understand, as a result of the saint's preaching, that the Catholic faith could be safely maintained against the Manichean attacks which until then he had supposed were unanswerable. This ended in his famous conversion.

It is not surprising that almost the moment after entering the Church St Augustine felt obliged to attack the Manicheism which had so long kept him, and no doubt was keeping many others, away from Christ. He wished first to tear from the "elect" the mask of "austerity", so attractive to the romanticism of every age. He wrote his treatise *On the Morals of the Catholic Church and Those of the Manicheans.* Then, immediately on his return to Africa, he composed his commentary on Genesis, *De Genesi contra Manichaeos,* in two books.

After becoming a priest he held two notable discussions with distinguished Manicheans, with Fortunatus on August 28th, 392, and with Felix in 404. The former fled from Hippo in his embarrassment, the latter embraced the Catholic faith. Next Augustine in a number of works turned to refuting their greatest authorities, Adimantus, Mani, Faustus of Milevis, with whom he had conversed at Carthage, and finally Secundinus. Besides these polemical writings he set out his thought on the subject of evil in three more general works: the treatises *On Free Will, On the Two Souls* and especially *On the Nature of Good* which seems to be the best summary of his anti-Manichean teaching.

It is from this last book that we take the main outlines of the Augustinian teaching about evil. At the start Augustine insists on the fact that the entire universe comes from God. The dictum *ab illo, non de illo* epitomizes the infinite distance which separates Christianity, with its teaching that God produced the world out of nothing, from all sorts of pantheism, including Manicheism, which would make God produce the world out of his own substance. "That which is *of* him is what he is: the things that are made *by* him are not what he is. Hence, if he alone is immutable, all things that he made, since he made them from nothing, are subject to change" (*De Natura Boni* 11).

In other words the condition of created existence is totally different from that of the creator. We have here a metaphysical principle. In this Augustine sees primarily an act of justice: "And because he is also just, he has not made the things he created of nothing equal to him whom he begat of himself" (*ibid.*).

All good things come from God, the greatest as well as the least. Some minds find it impossible to understand that every sort of being, material as well as spiritual, is good in itself. They are disturbed by the realization that a spirit can be evil and that the body is mortal. This leads them to postulate a dual nature, that of an evil spirit and a mortal body, originating elsewhere than from God. That is the Manichean position which Augustine attacks.

Everything good comes from God who has bestowed on his creatures measure, form and order (*modus, species, ordo*). The chief of these is order, namely the rational adaptation of creatures to their end. Order exists in the eternal truth, as the eternal law of all things. Its ultimate end is always in God. We share in this order if our way of life is leading us to God. We are outside this order if the behaviour we adopt leads us away from God. Measure is an aspect of order. The being which falls short of, or exceeds, the measure for which it was made is henceforth nothing, or something other than itself. So it is God who determines the measure of things. It is he who "has arranged all things *in measure, number and weight*" (Wisdom 11. 21). As for form, which corresponds to the "number" of Wisdom, it gives the creature its specification, that is, the place marked out for it in the scale of beings. All this comes from God. Where the measure, the form, the order, are great, there are great goods; where they are small the goods are small; where they are non-existent there is no longer any good at all.

Evil does not exist by itself. It is the corruption of measure, form and order. An evil nature is one that is corrupted. In so far as it is a nature, it is good; in so far as it is corrupted it becomes evil. We see that evil consists in corruption, that is, in breaking up (*rumpere*), in being deprived of what a being ought normally to possess. Only it must not be forgotten that a particular nature, albeit evil, albeit corrupted, may still outweigh in value another nature which has preserved its integrity. A rational spirit, corrupted by an evil will, would have greater value than an animal, even though perfect. A soul, however wicked, remains more valuable than the body to which it communicates life.

It was to the Platonists, as we gather from the *Confessions* (Bk. 7), that Augustine owed this solution of the problem of evil. Evil is not a being, but a privation of being, a limitation, a deficiency. It is a condition of the universal harmony. It has its origin in the free will of the rational creature: "To the most excellent of his creatures, namely, rational spirits, God has granted that they cannot be corrupted against their will, that is, if they remain obedient to the Lord their God, and thus cleave to his incorruptible beauty" (*De Natura Boni* 7).

But if they refuse to obey him and cleave to him in this way, order is re-established in another way, namely, by punishment: "For God is such a good that there is nothing good for him who leaves him; and among the things that God has made, a rational nature is so great a good, that no good can give it happiness, save only God" (*ibid.*).

Thus the Augustinian theory applies, not only to physical evil, but also to moral evil, to sin. The free, voluntary act can indeed be assimilated to a substance endowed with measure, form and order. If, in a given act, these perfections do not attain the degree proper to them, the act becomes evil, but the evil resides, not in the positive element retained in the act, but in its deficiency.

As for irrational creatures, their corruption actually contributes to the universal order. The less vigorous give way to the more vigorous, the weaker to the stronger, just as earthly things obey heavenly, as an inferior obeys his superior. The punishment of sin also contributes to order. If God pardons the penitent, it is a great act of generosity; if he punishes the guilty, there is no injustice done. Order is preserved better by a rational being's suffering justly inflicted punishment than by its practising sin with impunity. God, then, has not created evil, for only that which *is* can be created, and evil is pure nothingness, but God has brought every being out of nothingness, and every being brought out of nothingness is by that very fact corruptible. In so far as physical evil is concerned, the universe finds in the succession of beings, which cannot continue without the existence of corruption, an order, a balance and a beauty analogous to that of a poem or melody whose beauty is manifested not in space but in time.

Even the privations of things are so ordered in the natural universe, that the discerning mind may consider their changes not unbecoming. By withholding light from certain places and times God produces darkness no less agreeably than daylight. For if we, by restraining our voices, make an agreeable interval of silence in our speaking, how much more should he provide agreeably for certain things to suffer privation, like an artist designing all things in perfection. Therefore in the Hymn of

the Three Children (Daniel 3. 72) light and darkness also praise
God, that is, bring forth his praise in the hearts of those who
think well on them

(De Natura Boni 16)

Evil is not prime matter, as Mani alleged. Prime matter is
capable of receiving forms. If form is a good, there is no
doubt that the capacity for form is equally a good. Pain,
which many see as the greatest evil, can exist only in what is
naturally good. The element of resistance in suffering is, in a
sense, refusal to surrender the sort of being possessed, as
being something good. Distress of soul is caused by the resistance of the will to a superior power, pain of body by the
resistance of sense to a more powerful body. But painless
evils are worse. Better to suffer corruption than enjoy sin.
A painful wound is preferable to a hidden disease destroying
the body.

Moral evil poses a more delicate problem. For sin consists
not in desiring evil things, but in forgoing good things of a
higher order. Everything created by God is good. The tree of
the knowledge of good and evil was good in itself. But man,
when he touched it, gave up something better, namely, his
Creator, by desiring a created good against God's will. This
view corroborates and explains the Augustinian definition of
sin as *aversio a Deo, conversio ad creaturas*—turning away
from God and towards creatures. Sin lies, not in turning towards evil as an ultimate end, but in breaking away from the
order which directs us towards God. Evil for a created being
consists in the diminution of good, namely, of measure, form
and order. If God forbade the touching of the tree of knowledge of good and evil, it was to show that the nature of the
rational soul was not at its own disposal but needed to submit
to God. Thus, it is by obedience that it preserves the right
order of its salvation, and by disobedience it breaks this order.
The sinner makes an evil use of a good, namely, of his freedom. God makes a good use of the evil, re-establishing order

by the punishment he inflicts on the sinner. The very eternal
fire which torments the wicked is not evil in itself. It has
measure, form and order. Suffering is an evil for the damned,
but it is due to their sin. Light is not evil because it gives pain
to diseased eyes.

Augustine proceeds to criticize the dualism of the Manicheans. He has no difficulty in showing that the Manicheans
attribute to what they call the principle of evil such goods as
life, power, sentience, light, attractiveness, measure, form and
order, and that in what they call the supreme good, they
admit the presence of death, sickness, forgetfulness, stupidity,
etc. As for the consequences their doctrine leads to in morals
they are as vicious as they are senseless.

We can carry the problem still further and ask if the freedom which permits the choice of evil is of itself a good. Of
itself, Augustine replies, it is inferior as a good to the perfect
freedom enjoyed by the elect, and even to the grace of liberty
which was the lot of Adam in the earthly Paradise. But free
will, however imperfect, is the condition of the greatest good
that can befall us, the happiness of heaven. Man can abuse it.
All evil consists in that. No doubt by his grace God could
have prevented the evil choices of our free will. Yet it is not
he who is the cause of evil, but our will which freely forsakes
God. Moreover, to put right this disorder for which he is in
no way responsible, God comes to our aid and creates anew
by grace the order lost by sin. This is not to destroy freedom,
but to enhance it. Nothing can have greater freedom than
free will when it can no longer enslave itself to sin (cf. *De
Corrept. et Gratia*, 4). It is the crowning of one good by
another still greater.

Although living in the thirteenth century, in a completely
Christian environment, St Thomas Aquinas also came to grips
with the problem of evil. In fact it was preaching to counter
the Albigensian heresy, a later form of Manicheism, which

provided the occasion for St Dominic's founding the Order of Preachers. St Thomas gives the subject special treatment in the *De Malo*, the second of the *Quaestiones Disputatae*. The first question he asks deals with the reality of evil. Is it something positive or mere privation? One is tempted to see in it a positive fact, since it is the contrary of good. Black is a colour as much as white. Moreover it is held that contraries belong to the same genus. But he quickly establishes that the term *malum* can signify either of two things: an evil creature, or simply the quality of evil. The evil being is a reality, but not the quality of evil. It is mere privation of a particular good. It is only good that is desired and desirable. It is a reality which comes from the supreme reality, which is the infinitely desirable good. But evil does not come from the supreme reality. Everything created by God is necessarily a particular, and therefore limited, good. It is good to the extent that it *is*, it is evil in the degree to which it lacks something. If evil existed in itself, it would desire nothing, nor would it be the object of any desire, and would accordingly have no activity. On the other hand being of itself is a good: all beings desire to maintain themselves in the degree of being which they possess. Nothing desires not to be. Blindness is a not-being, a mere privation. In reality, what exists is the blind man, although he does not enjoy the full possession of his normal endowment.

Evil is either absolute or relative. A thing is evil in itself when it lacks a perfection its nature requires. Illness is of itself an evil, because man is made to enjoy health. But an object can possess all the qualities that go to make up its being and still be evil in relation to something else. Fire and water are both good, but each is bad for the other. Similarly, justice, though good in itself, can deprive a given sinner of a good which he would naturally possess. Punishment is good and just in itself, but bad for the sinner. We say that God creates hell, but that he makes peace. In the first case there is no cooperation of desire on the part of the sinner. In the second there is cooperation, in that man desires the peace which God gives him.

St Thomas then asks whether the subject in which evil exists is good. He explains that "good" has three different meanings. It can be used to express a thing's perfection: great keenness of vision is good for the eye. Virtue is good for man. It can also be said of the subject which possesses this perfection: a good eye is one which has keen vision. A good man is one who possesses virtue. But it can also be said of that which is potentially perfect: man is good because he can acquire virtue. The eye is good because it can attain to keenness of vision. But here there is room for evil, if we suppose that the being which is potentially good is actually deprived of a perfection it should possess. It is good to be potentially good. It is bad to remain in potency when one should be in act. It is bad for a man who could become virtuous to remain without virtue, or for an eye which could with care become keen to remain sightless. Evil is potency for good remaining idle when it should pass into act. It follows that God, who is pure act, that is, has no potency requiring act to complete it, is also the perfect good. There is therefore no contradiction between evil and the good subject, but rather between evil and the perfection the subject ought to possess.

It can even be said, in spite of the Gospel saying "A good tree does not produce evil fruit", that evil can only come from good, or, with Pseudo-Dionysius, that the beginning and end of all evils is the good. Of course, that is only a manner of speaking: evil as such cannot have a positive cause. In the first place it is not desired for its own sake: what the adulterer desires is not injustice but love. Secondly, effects necessarily preserve some sort of resemblance to the causes that produce them, whereas evil has no resemblance with the being that occasions it. Lastly, a cause is always to some extent made for the production of its effect, while good has in no sense been created for the production of evil.

However, if evil finds a positive cause neither in being nor in goodness, it does find a negative, or accidental, cause in them. This can happen for two reasons: first, because the good which causes an evil is always deficient, and secondly because the good which causes an evil does not regard the evil as its goal. It aims at something good without directly willing the evil effect. Thus, when a man commits adultery, he aims solely at his pleasure without taking account either of justice or of the sanctity of marriage. This is a moral evil, a wrong in the proper sense. He is responsible for this evil because his will could accept or reject it. But his will does not approach the evil except in so far as it brings with it a particular good, it does not approach it because it is evil. It would not do so unless it was deficient in some respect, namely, in failing to consider that its act was contrary to the divine will. A joiner, through not having his rule always at hand, might cut his wood too short because he worked by rule of thumb and did not spare the time to check his measurements. His work would be bad work. But whereas the joiner's apprentice is capable of keeping his rule at hand while he works, the will has not the strength always to keep the divine will in view so as never to lose the exact measurement. In this it does not sin. It sins when it makes a choice of some importance without reference to its rule. It is thus the cause of evil while remaining good in itself—only the accidental cause, first because it has not willed it directly, and secondly, on account of its deficiency in forgetting to have recourse to its rule.

The divine will, on the other hand, cannot sin, for it is itself the rule of its action. It has no need to refer to another rule.

St Thomas then asks another question: is there a real distinction between the evil of wrongdoing and that of punishment? Obviously he is only concerned here with evil in so far as it affects rational beings. To undergo punishment presupposes having incurred responsibility. The evil of wrong-doing lies in the direction of the will of the man who commits it; the evil of punishment is on the contrary opposed to the will of the man who undergoes it: "The tradition of faith holds that the rational creature can undergo no punishment, whether in respect of soul or body or exterior possessions, unless sin, proper either to the person or to his nature, has gone before. It thus follows that all privation of such good as can profitably be used by men is called punishment; and the same argument is valid in the case of angels. And so all evil for rational creatures falls under the heading either of wrong-doing or of punishment" (*De Malo*, q.I. a.4. corp.).

Not all punishment is opposed to the will in the same way. Some is opposed to a will that is conscious of the fact, for example, when the offender knows that he is receiving his punishment. Other punishment opposes the will without its realizing it. This is the case when a man, as a result of wrong-doing, receives an injury of which he is unaware, but which he would deplore if he knew about it. Finally there are evils which are only opposed to a rightly ordered will, for instance, the loss of the virtue of charity in one who has committed a mortal sin. More often than not the evil of wrongdoing consists in an action, whereas the evil of punishment is under-gone passively.

Finally, St Thomas discusses the question whether the greatest evil is that of wrongdoing or that of punishment.

From a superficial point of view the question presents no difficulty. If one considers bodily punishment only, it is clear that wrongdoing is a greater evil than punishment. It is neces-sary, however, to take a wider view. Loss of sanctifying grace and the glory of heaven is itself a punishment. And it is opposed to the possession of the sovereign good, which consti-tutes man's ultimate end.

Nevertheless it must be held that wrongdoing is a greater evil than punishment. In the first place it is wrongdoing that places man in the state of being deprived of grace and glory; next, wrongdoing is more opposed to God than punishment which is at least in accordance with his justice; moreover the way to avoid punishment is to flee from sin; finally, wrongdoing is an action while punishment has a passive character. In other words, wrongdoing separates from the love of God, punishment from the enjoyment of God.

It follows that it is better to refrain from evil for fear of doing wrong than for fear of punishment. St Thomas recalls Horace's words:

> *Oderunt peccare mali formidine poenae,*
> *Oderunt peccare boni virtutis amore.*[1]

It is important to notice the background of St Thomas' study of evil. He devoted five years' disputations to it between 1263 and 1268. But, out of sixteen *quaestiones*, only the first is devoted to evil in general. He follows this by a long discussion of sin, the only real evil and the cause of all other evils: the essence of sin; its causes: the devil, ignorance, weakness, malice; then original sin and the punishment it incurs. Before beginning to study actual sin, he discusses man's freedom in an article which constitutes by itself the sixth question. Then he passes to venial sin. Next, he begins to study the capital sins, vainglory, envy, accidie or spiritual listlessness, anger, avarice, gluttony, lust. He ends with a question in twelve articles on evil spirits, which provides an excellent conclusion to his treatise.

In other words, for him the problem of evil takes its place amid a vast setting. The same thing appears in the pages of the *Summa*. In discussing the fall, the redemption, man's freedom, man's elevation by grace, actual grace, St Thomas step

---

[1] "The wicked dislike doing wrong for fear of punishment; the good dislike doing wrong for love of virtue." This is how St Thomas gives the quotation (*De Malo* I. 5 ad xi). What Horace actually wrote was: *Oderunt peccare boni virtutis amore: tu nihil admittes in te formidine poenae.* (*Epp.* I. 16. 52.) (*Trans..*)

by step solves the enigma of evil. It might almost be said that the entire Christian religion exists solely to lift man and the rest of creation out of the evil into which they have fallen.

With St Thomas, Christian thought on the subject of evil reached its full elaboration. A few details needed adding, but they did nothing to change the idea as a whole. We can therefore pass now to the exposition of theological teaching on the subject of evil.

PART III

THEOLOGY

CHAPTER VII

EVIL

The work of analysis we have done in collecting what revelation has to tell us in holy Scripture and Catholic tradition would be sufficient to give a complete knowledge of the teaching on the subject. But theology is not just a catalogue of sources, it is a rational process of working out what is given in revelation. It should offer us a rigorously exact exposition of the teaching of faith—that is the first thing that is asked of it—but, by making use of philosophical methods, it should also provide a synthesis to satisfy the human intellect's need for unity and comprehension. Theology has not always existed in the Church. The first need was to preach the coming of God's kingdom among men. But since the first centuries there has been an attempt at methodical exposition combined with scientific and philosophical interpretation adapted to the general culture of the age. The thirteenth century gave birth to a most brilliant development of theology, still capable of arousing our admiration. But the unifying work of theology will never be completed. It needs revising and reshaping in every age inasmuch as there is a constant change of intellectual requirements. It would be a mistake to give children nothing but a catechetical summary without putting them in touch with the word of God. Equally, it would be wrong to present adults with a detailed analysis of revelation without trying to adapt this teaching to the needs of a more open mind interested in a comprehensive study. This is what this third part attempts to do.

First of all there is a piece of advice on which we must insist; its usefulness is unquestionable. This inquiry should be undertaken and pursued in a calm and peaceful spirit. When we are racked with suffering it is precisely not the time to examine its *raisons d'être*. St James says in his epistle, "Is one of you unhappy? Let him fall to prayer" (James 5. 13). He will quickly find in contact with God the consolation and strength he needs. He would not find them in argumentation incapable of changing reality. This applies even to the study of a theological account of the matter. When Bossuet on his deathbed was enduring the agony caused by the stone "as big as your egg", he had read to him, not a passage of the *Summa Theologica* or the wonderful sermons in which he himself had vindicated divine Providence, but, as many as sixty times over, the priestly prayer of Christ in St John's Gospel (17). He felt himself calmed by the intentions Christ revealed to his Father before proceeding to his suffering and death. If, to cast off his anxiety about his salvation, he had tried instead to reflect on the mystery of predestination, he would have found only harsher torment and deeper obscurity. Theological reflection is extremely useful in nourishing and strengthening faith, but only in periods of calm, when there is complete peace of mind and deep-seated happiness. In times of trouble and suffering it is necessary to turn rather to deep and heart-felt prayer.

It is all the more urgent to recall that we live in days when men's nerves, subject to continual and powerful excitement, have a more acute sensitivity. That does not mean that evil must be studied with a heart of iron and forehead of brass, but only that we should try to keep a well-balanced sensibility and remain masters of our imagination. If man were in his primitive state, that is, in the same order as was his at his creation, with the sensitive faculties under the control of the intellectual, the imagination subject to the intellect, and the sense-appetite to the will, the problem of evil would scarcely arise. But it is so no longer. We must take care not to increase the real distress we feel at present by an over-vivid imagination and an exaggerated tendency to emotion.

In consequence of the progress made by medicine now fighting most successfully to overcome physical pain, and in consequence, too, of the terrifying evils our age has witnessed, above all in the two world wars, we have become extremely sensitive to suffering, and especially bodily suffering. On the other hand, for want, no doubt, of a religious sense, moral evil, sin, does not horrify us as it did the saints. So it is important to redress the balance and reestablish the true dimensions of the mystery before making any judgement.

What then is evil in itself? It is as difficult for us to form an idea of evil as to form an idea of nothingness. Because of the impossibility of thinking without accompanying our intellectual representation with images of seeing, hearing or touching, nothingness becomes a sort of being for us. We try to form an idea, of the vaguest possible kind, of empty space. But even space is being. Our intellect has then to exclude by an effort of abstraction the element of falsehood introduced by the image accompanying our idea. In fact we cannot form an idea of nothingness except by comparison with, or by opposition to, being.

It is the same with the idea of ugliness. It is not intelligible in itself, but only by comparison with the idea of beauty. This is shown by the fact that it is entirely relative, that, for example, the ape which is beautiful among animals is ugly in comparison with man. Ugliness is simply lack of beauty, a deficiency in proportion and order. Similarly, evil is not being, not anything positive, but simply the privation of a good. It is no evil for a man not to have wings. His nature is complete without them. It has no need of flying equipment. Evil is a privation, that is, the absence of a quality due to the nature of a being, but in fact lacking. *Bonum ex integra causa, malum ex quocumque defectu.* This privation is a disorder, and since order is the rational adaptation of means to end, it can attach to the end or the means.

To the end: a bad cook is one who cannot or will not cook well. A bad motor is one incapable of transmitting motion to the mechanism dependent on it. A bad horse is one which cannot carry its rider or draw its vehicle. It is for good cooking that one has a cook, for transmitting motion that one has a motor, for the saddle or the traces that one uses a horse.

Privation can attach to means ill-adapted to the purpose for which they are intended. My eye is bad if the crystalline lens is incapable of adapting its volume to the distance of the object I am looking at, my oven is bad if its heat cannot be regulated to bake things in the way desired, a shelter is bad if it cannot protect me from cold and inclemency.

Sometimes it happens that the privation is purely imaginary, in the sense that something may appear to lack a thing due to its nature, when it is only due to custom. A small boy is very miserable about not having a bicycle if all his friends have been given one. A housewife considers it a misfortune to be without a washing-machine, because all her friends and neighbours have one. A motorist is annoyed to have to run in his car, not thinking that a hundred years ago no one had achieved the speed of forty miles an hour, which he today considers so slow.

But not all evils are imaginary. Although it is only a privation, evil really exists. It arises from acts whose value is morally deficient, through their not being related to God, the ultimate end of the universe and of man in particular. Like a grain of sand in the delicate works of a machine, this way of acting introduces into the cosmos a disorder which can have incalculable consequences. There are other acts which fall below their proper standard through a failure to use the means imposed by the moral law or those alone capable of achieving the purpose in view. This too is a disorder which can have endless repercussions.

As for physical evil, it is useless to steel oneself against it like the Stoics, or to deny its existence like the Christian Scientists. The first cry a baby utters at birth is provoked by suffering. He will have to suffer right up to his last breath. Doubtless there will be degrees of suffering. All the same it will be real. And the more he tries, from weakness, to escape evil, the more refined his sensitivity will become, so that he will come to feel sensations and emotions which a more hardened person would not notice.

When the evils a person has to endure are of the common sort—childhood illnesses, difficulties of adolescence, family bereavements, difficulties in making a career, old age, disease and death—they scarcely seem to be evils. They are part, so to speak, of man's nature, and to see them as evil we need to be reminded by faith that man was not created in this state. But with extraordinary evils—rare and painful disease, accidents, estrangement within families, premature bereavement—it seems far worse. We feel we have been deprived of what was normally due to human nature. Then there exist unthinkable sufferings, situations, by human standards, beyond hope. Here we may simply recall the Nazi concentration camps. A witness writes:

> I realized that it was not a question of lack of order or failure of organization, but that it was on the contrary a fully developed, conscious idea that had presided over the setting up of the camp. We had been condemned to die in our own dirt, to be swamped in filth, in our own excrement. The intention was to bring us low, to humiliate the human dignity in us, to efface in us every trace of humanity, to reduce us to the level of wild beasts, to inspire us with a horror and a distrust of ourselves and our fellows. This was the aim, this was the

idea! The Germans were perfectly aware of all this. They knew that we should be unable to view each other without disgust.[1]

One can understand how Malebranche, hearing the evil that exists in the world compared to the shadows skilfully distributed in a picture or the discords which maintain movement within harmony, found this way of speaking detestable. "Shadows are necessary in a painting and discords in music, and is it therefore necessary that women should miscarry and produce an infinity of monsters? A fine inference!"[2]

Evil is an evil. It has to be accepted and presented as such in its terrible reality. Only we must be careful not to attribute anything positive to it. It is a good thing to move about. It is a bad thing to move about with a limp, but it is a lesser evil than not moving about at all. Thus evil is always inherent in a subject that is good in itself, but has not all the perfection intended for it.

We must not lose sight of the fact that the existence of God is logically prior to the problem of evil. The existence even of an imperfect world, even of a world full of evil, is inexplicable unless it has its origin in a perfect being. An imperfect being, however great, however powerful, would not suffice. There cannot be any defect in the Creator, nor any potency even, in the philosophical sense of the term, if he is to be wholly and completely in act.

And this supremely perfect being could not create a world equal to himself in perfection. Such a world would be indistinguishable from himself. He could only create a finite world and, however beautiful it might be, there would be room in this world for evil.

Ought it then to be created? Obviously, the solution of this problem is in the divine wisdom and infinitely surpasses our understanding. Nevertheless, we must try to penetrate into

---

[1] Mme Lewinska, *Vingt mois à Auschwitz*, p. 61.
[2] Third letter in reply to the first book of Reflections of M. Arnauld.

this plan of creation. We are well aware that we shall not understand everything, but to know the least thing of God is worth more than knowing the whole world perfectly. In humility, as befits the children of God, we shall try, however imperfect our view, to see why God has permitted evil.

CHAPTER VIII

SIN AND EVIL

Modern writers usually make a distinction between physical evil and moral evil. St Thomas' insight went further and deeper when he placed the distinction between the evil of wrongdoing and that of punishment. To be deprived of God is certainly a moral evil, but it is not the evil of sin.

The evil of wrongdoing is the result of a divergence between the will of a rational created being and the will of God. It is a revolt against the absolute sovereignty of the Creator. It is an act of rashness, if the sinner imagines he will escape from God's justice or the justice that is immanent in God's ordering of the world. It is a disorder knowingly introduced into the harmony of the universe. Irrational created beings are radically incapable of producing such a disorder. The sky, with its depth surpassing all imagining, arrayed splendidly with its stars, sings God's glory. All unconsciously it repeats the "music of the spheres". It sings, for no other reason than that it exists. The life of plants which burst forth, grow, produce flowers and fruit to prolong their generations to infinity, though distant and rudimentary, is nevertheless a reflection of the life of God. It reveals in some measure the beauty of that life.

The animal creation too speaks of the variety of the divine ideas and adds to the beauty of a world enlivened by its power of movement. But, though they have a certain knowledge of themselves, they have no responsibility for what they do, for they realize only its material side.

Wholly different is the condition of man. Man sees the world in a double light. Eve considers the fruit of the tree of knowledge of good and evil. Materially, considered in isolation from other things, it is beautiful, delightful. Its scent, its colour give a hint of its pleasant taste. At the same time she recalls the meaning of her action. It constitutes an act of disobedience to God; or, more simply, it is for her a deadly fruit, since she is aware of God's threat. It is by measuring these two realizations one against the other that human liberty is made possible, that man is saddled with moral responsibility.

It is man's duty to contribute to the glory of God, but not only in the manner of the lower orders of creation. Doubtless he does contribute in this way in the first place; but he should do it also willingly and freely. He makes his way thus towards his own happiness, a happiness which transcends him, which he cannot attain by himself, which he could not even believe possible, but which he awaits according to God's promise. This happiness he receives from God, but it needs his co-operation. Always there is the impossibility—it is the very mystery of created being—of being bracketed with God. All the glory of man's salvation returns to God who has accomplished everything. On his side, man, who himself too has accomplished it all, shares in the glory of God without lessening that glory.

What is true of our gaining glory is true of each of our acts, from the greatest to the least. God's assistance is responsible for all that is being, all that is positive, in the act. If the act is bad, if it falls short of the perfection it should have, God's assistance will have been responsible only for the positive part, he will have taken no share in the evil, which belongs to non-being. For that man alone bears the whole responsibility. If the act is good, God will have assisted completely and right up to the end. God cannot be the cause of anything but what is being, what is positive, what is perfect.

It must be added that man was not made to live by himself. He is a social being. Even should he withdraw himself artificially from the society of his fellows, he would still, in spite of himself, be a part of it. And this fact gives his acts a universal significance which is not limited by the human race. Most of the time this influence is trifling. All acts do not affect the human race like the sin of Adam, who bore the responsibility for all his descendants, like the passion of Christ who offered satisfaction to God for the whole of humanity. These are extreme cases, the limiting instances, which are, nevertheless, inexplicable without there being in the entire human race a solidarity in respect of good and evil. Many individual crimes have very distant consequences. The crime of an ancestor can cause in one of his descendants a dangerous atavism, an unfortunate heredity. The cruelty of a father in deserting his wife and children will cause the misery of a whole family. A fortune squandered will result in children born in poverty where they will be for ever deprived of the up-bringing and education that was their due. Often, like the concentric waves which develop in water when a stone is thrown into it, the consequences of a crime propagate themselves in unforeseen ways. Conversely, good acts create an atmosphere of uprightness and moral strength. As Elisabeth Leseur wrote, "every soul which raises itself up raises up the world".

It follows that the liberty of each individual influences to a greater or lesser extent the liberty of all, and not only by way of advice or example, but by changing the circumstances of life. In the natural order these circumstances accepted by society can be modified by new needs, new inventions. In the supernatural order account must be taken of the merit *de congruo*[1] of each member of the Church for his brothers, the prayer or suffering of a privileged soul. Nevertheless, this liberty which is subject to so many influences does not disappear. It remains intact in each individual, aided rather than hampered by the enlightenment received by the intellect as well as by the gentle attraction of grace. Indeed we have here two crucial points, two encounters which bring the whole of life into place and where life attains its greatest intensity.

It cannot be gainsaid that this liberty entails some awkward consequences. It can choose between acting and not acting. It can also choose between one way of acting and another, but in either of the choices the moral order is brought into play. Not acting can be evil, as disordered as acting in a way forbidden by the moral law. In other words, liberty can choose evil. This is not the essence of liberty. It is an imperfection of liberty. But it is a fact of experience. In heaven, although remaining free, the elect will no longer be able to choose evil, but only to opt between different goods. Being unable to lose touch with the supreme good, they will be unable to cut themselves off from it. Here on earth the choice between good and evil remains open. Not that free will can choose evil *as* evil. Evil, which belongs to not-being, has nothing which can draw things to it. But free will can choose a particular good which is opposed to a higher good, namely, the order which we ought to keep in regard to God, our ultimate end.

The will only chooses evil if it has for an instant at least lost touch with the thought of a higher good. Such a distraction can bring about a small wrongdoing. There is no wrongdoing even in small matters unless faith has undergone some momentary diminution. In our actual life it is inevitable there should be many such distractions. God only asks of us not to

---

[1] Merit *de congruo* is distinguished from merit *de condigno*. By the latter God's justice obliges him to reward us, by the former the reward is due only to a sense of fitness. Members of the Body of Christ can only merit for each other *de congruo*. (*Trans.*)

accept them definitively, to recover ourselves when we realize what we are doing, to tend always to become better. This weakness keeps us in humility, in consciousness of the necessity of grace, in the spirit of prayer.

Sad to say, more serious sins are committed. It happens that the will imposes silence on the understanding, so that considerations of faith—or in the case of pagans the dictates of conscience—are as far as possible kept away. At the same time the will forces the attention towards the particular good that it desires, in such a way that all attraction is reserved for this good to the exclusion of the moral good. Then self-love, in the words of St Augustine, comes to the point of despising God and his law. Here we are in the fullness of moral evil. If the object desired becomes truly opposed to the ultimate end, there is a rupture with God, mortal sin, that is to say the greatest evil that can be. Man has turned aside from his goal. He strays in disorder, at the prompting of his self-will.

In the case of a Christian, he has broken his baptismal promises, he has shut charity out from his soul, he has ceased to be the temple of the living God. He is a branch snapped off the divine tree, a branch liable to be thrown into the fire since it has lost its usefulness. What is more, he has introduced disorder into the divine handiwork. Creation must of necessity turn against him.

It is clear that the freedom to choose in this way between good and evil brings with it an immense drawback: every act of will which decides for evil adds to the evil which already exists in the world. And there is the possibility of damnation, of beings whom death has fixed for eternity in disorder, because their souls did not believe in love, did not want love.

If man is to be placed in such responsibility, at a cross-roads fraught with such great danger, the compensating advantages must be incomparable. Otherwise God would never have chosen such a state of affairs. His goodness assures us of that. Without altogether understanding it, we see at least that he wishes the rational beings he created, men as well as angels, to share in determining their own destiny. He has left them, not only the burden, but also the glory, of choosing. He has matched the difficulty of the struggle by the beauty of the crown, but above all he has allowed the consciousness of the created being to decide for itself through love of him. Moreover, he who has no need of anything or anyone, whose real glory cannot be added to, desires the homage of a freedom which gives itself spontaneously, a homage which is the greatest extrinsic glory he can receive from his creation.

So greatly does God prize this liberty, that he finds divine means of aiding, sustaining, even of diverting it, without ever violating it or imposing himself on it directly. This demands astonishing control, because God, who is the supreme and unique good, has only to show himself to incline the will of necessity towards himself. Moreover, being Omnipotence, he has only to speak for everything to be created. Nothing can resist his will. But his will is precisely that man should be free:

> Do not complain that it was he led thee into false paths;
>> What need has God, thinkest thou, of rebels?
> No foul misdeed there is but God hates it;
>> There is no loving it and fearing him.
> When, men first came to be, it was God made them,
>> And, making them, left them to the arbitrament of their own wills;
> Yet giving them commandments to be their rule.
> Those commandments if thou wilt observe,
>> They in their turn shall preserve thee,
>> And give thee warrant of his favour.
> It is as though he offered thee fire and water,
>> Bidding thee take which thou wouldst;
> Life and death, blessing and curse, man finds set before him,
>> And the gift given thee shall be the choice thou makest.

(Ecclus 15. 12–18.)

It is necessary therefore that God should make himself known without showing himself, by means of a knowledge that is absolutely certain without being obvious, which remains obscure although it provides firm guidance. This is faith. While introducing man into the supernatural order, that is, putting him on the road that will lead to participation in the happiness of God, faith, nevertheless, by its very obscurity, leaves his heart the liberty of directing its love. Even mystical knowledge, based on the gifts of wisdom and understanding, respects the obscurity of faith and preserves for the soul its liberty of choosing between good and evil. A few privileged souls have been confirmed in grace and no longer have the power to choose evil. Even amongst the saints this is utterly exceptional. They are thus kept in humility of heart and helped to attribute their salvation and sanctification to God alone, in the thought that of themselves they are capable of nothing but evil.

Moreover, to help and strengthen the will, God has chosen grace, an entity difficult to imagine let alone describe, whose praises Scripture seems to sing when it praises Wisdom: "Mind-enlightening is the influence that dwells in her; set high apart; one in its source, yet manifold in its operation, subtle, yet easily understood. An influence quick in movement, unassailable, persuasive, gentle, right-thinking, keen-edged, irresistible, beneficent, kindly, proof against all error and all solicitude" (Wisdom 7. 22)—gentle enough to avoid force, strong enough to lead the soul to sanctity.

It is enough to recognize that if freedom is able to bring evil into the world, it nevertheless offers marvellous possibilities for the glory of God and the happiness of man.

CHAPTER IX

EVIL AND PUNISHMENT

Bergson remarks that the problem of evil depends in great measure on the sort of idea we have of God. We should no more picture God as a sort of doting grandpapa than as a cold-hearted bureaucrat who keeps his records with a total absence of feeling; still less should we see him as a torturer who obtains satisfaction from inflicting cruel punishments. He is infinitely merciful, he does not wish the death of a sinner but that he should be converted, he does not willingly assist in the loss of a soul. On the other hand he is infinitely just. The laws he has decreed remain in force both in the physical and in the moral order and, while retaining the power to modify or suspend them, he does so seldom, and only for the most serious reasons.

The primary moral law is that the rational creature is subjected to a test, a test which, however, has a time-limit. For the angels one instant was enough. The depth and amplitude of their intelligence was such as to enable them to take in at a glance the question of their acceptance or rejection of grace. In addition to an excellence of nature surpassing our own spiritual endowment, they were raised up to a new level, a participation in the divine life, and this in a measure exactly corresponding to their natural superiority. But this exaltation, by which they could win a share in the eternal happiness of God, was a free gift. It was an act of God's goodness requiring their acceptance. God wished to deify them, but he forbade them, as he forbade every creature, to wish to usurp the divine likeness on their own. One instant was enough to decide their response. But this response was fixed for always.

We men are liable to go back on our decisions because of lack of information. The angelic world is without this infirmity. The response they made to God determined the angels' destiny for eternity. There was no going back on it.

For man the conditions are different. His reason only awakens slowly, his conscience has to be trained to find its balance. Accordingly, his testing-time is prolonged. Man is thus able to re-make his life several times over, to be converted, that is, to turn back to God, though previously having abandoned the pursuit of his ultimate end. Only the length of the duration of this test is unknown. We know neither where, nor when, nor how death will overtake us. But the process must have an end, and this end must come while we are still dependent on faith, so that our freedom of choice remains intact. It would be too easy to make the decisive choice in the presence of God. No one could turn from a higher good to choose one that was lower and incomplete. There would be no test in that case. On the other hand, if we knew in advance how long we had to go, we would be liable to live presumptuously and without love, and intend postponing the choice until the moment of death. These arrangements are very wise, but it is obvious that God, once he had determined on them, would not call them into question. No one is truly responsible and liable to God's judgement unless he has had a chance of choosing consciously between good and evil, between seeking God and rejecting him. But it is possible that this choice should incur guilt. Man has only himself to blame.

Another moral law lays down that no disorder can be introduced into the universe which the hands of God have made without bringing in its train evil and suffering, not by way of vindictiveness on God's part, but because the fixity of the laws of nature require it. An obstruction thrown clumsily into the works of a machine is enough to ruin the whole mechanism. The machine was planned to function only when perfectly clean. It cannot produce the same results when hampered by something that fouls it. The same is true of the world. The first lie created a lack of trust among men, which will always persist, and which has caused quantities of further lies. The man who begets a child when drunk is in danger of giving life to a being that is maladjusted, rickety or destined for insanity. The man who through megalomania or timidity lets loose a war might find himself accountable for the tears, bereavements and disorders that result from it.

Why does God allow these things? Because he could only stop them by a miracle, that is, by a manifest violation of the laws of nature. Miracles are possible, of course, but only in a religious context, as a means of appending God's signature to a doctrine of revealed truth, of showing God's favour towards a particular enterprise, or of bringing to light the sanctity of a particular person. But to believe that God intervenes every moment to rectify the blunders of men responsible for their acts and the consequences of their acts is ignorance of his nature. He has created a world that is intelligible. Were he to be continually modifying the laws of nature, the human mind would get lost in its study of the world, and man could no longer gain control of the material world by scientific and technical skill, as he is intended to do. If God had overthrown the laws of atomic fission at the moment of the bomb's falling on Hiroshima, it would have become impossible for man to turn nuclear energy to his use.

It is true enough that God could have made evil descend solely on those who are guilty, but had he done so it would still have been by a miracle, by a violation of that law of moral solidarity mentioned earlier, which in the natural order is the basis of the mystery of redemption. Moreover, if punishment fell uniquely and regularly on the author of evil, the obscurity of faith would disappear together with freedom of choice and merit. We should no more do good for the love of the invisible God, who is, nevertheless, present, but through fear of a sword of Damocles for ever hanging over us, and this would rob the acts of human beings of practically all moral value.

It is true that the laws of nature, like freedom, can have disadvantages. Undeserved evil descending on the innocent can become a stumbling-block. It can give the irreligious ground for believing that life is nothing but a game where chance holds sway, that they can carry on without rule or guidance following the whim of their blind desires. It can also give superficial minds the impression that the world is in continual disorder, that it is senseless, that being is irrational, unrestricted by cause and necessity. What is still more serious, suffering which, at least in appearance, is undeserved can bring the person who undergoes it terrible temptations to discouragement and despair. Our Lord's cry at the moment of death, "My God, my God, why hast thou forsaken me?" shows that he too struck this dangerous reef, but by his very dereliction he obtained the necessary help for these souls. God does not allow his children to be tempted beyond their strength. He brings them out of temptation, giving them the power to overcome it (1 Cor. 10. 13). But one must have seen men and women floundering amid inextricable and inescapable difficulties without knowing the reason for these trials, in order to understand the agony these souls experience. The benefits, the good side, of suffering which we are now to consider do not alter the fact that it is an evil in itself and can sometimes bring with it terrible dangers. Our Lord taught us to say, not only "Forgive us our trespasses", but also "Lead us not into temptation, but deliver us from evil".

CHAPTER X

THE BENEFITS OF EVIL:

PREVENTION

Clearly, in talking of the advantages or benefits of evil there can be no question of a positive contribution which evil itself has to offer. It must be repeated that evil is only non-being and privation. What is meant is that God, in permitting evil, finds means of giving added being, beauty and goodness to the spiritual world, and thereby to the world as a whole. It is a law even at the natural level: limited being, if it is artificially constricted, condenses and accumulates energy it can later discharge. A dam, by producing a change of level and temporarily arresting the flow of water, enables a power-station to provide a vast amount of electric current. Left to itself a fruit-tree will spread its branches in any and every direction and produce an abundance of foliage. The gardener, who wants fruit, prunes the tree. To all appearance he is doing extensive damage. In reality he is only cutting back branches greedy for sap and making the whole force of the sap concentrate on the branches that will bear fruit. Perhaps this does not benefit the tree, but it benefits the gardener, the consumer of the fruit.

In the same way God can use evil which, viewed absolutely, is merely a contraction of being, to obtain greater effectiveness and greater beauty. It is only in this sense that one can talk of the advantages of evil, suffering and even sin. Nevertheless these advantages are very real and abundantly outweigh the existing evil.

The first advantage which God can bring out of evil is to use it as a warning to prevent a more serious evil. This is, in fact, the primary rôle of physical pain. When a part of the body receives an injury, it usually manifests itself, if internal, by physical suffering in the form of pain. It can hardly be said to constitute an evil. It is the danger-signal coming into action. It is indispensable, for if there were nothing but pleasure to attract us to do the things necessary for our life we should easily forget the more important points. One pleasure makes us forget another. A real reader rarely bothers to take his meals. Pain is much more effective. It can indeed be deadened for an instant. It does not stop making itself felt until it has received satisfaction. It is not a good thing to be insensitive to injuries. We need only think of certain painless types of cancer. Pain becomes an evil when the danger-signal goes wrong. At that point it becomes useless, no longer providing any useful warning. Fortunately the various methods of analgesia make it possible to combat it at this stage.

It is also an evil when it prevents beneficial treatment of disease. Early surgical operations found pain their great obstacle. The patient's defensive reactions prevented that muscular "relaxation" which allows the surgeon to operate smoothly for as long as is necessary without damaging the tissues. Thanks to anaesthesia this has become possible and surgery has been able to achieve gigantic progress in a very short time.

To speak more generally, it must be admitted that the benefit we receive from pain is much greater than the harm it does us. We have acquired, especially the white races, a keenness of nervous perception which makes us extremely sensitive to pain, but science has meanwhile put at our disposal sedatives of great efficacy to mitigate or suppress excessive pain.

With some exceptions the same may be said of animal suffering. The first point to notice is that the animal nervous system is less delicate than the human. An equivalent stimulus causes them less suffering than it would human beings. Also, with man, an intelligent being, pain frequently gives rise to a host of questions: what organ is affected? What is the cause? Will the pain get worse or better? Am I to expect similar attacks from now on, or is it pure accident? Is this pain an indication that there is danger of death? Does it portend a long illness? What is to become of me if I cannot go on working? At the first attack especially, the human sufferer has more to endure from these questionings than from the actual pain he feels.

These questions do not arise for the animal. It suffers without realization and without anguish. The pain often gives it a warning which puts it on its guard against something that could hurt it. The only case where an animal can experience more acute suffering is when man interferes with it maliciously. There we are once more in the presence of moral evil with its repercussions in the lower orders of creation.

Another evil which serves as a warning is remorse of conscience. It is, however, suffering of a special sort, since it does not last long. The conscience quickly becomes hardened to reproaches when it refuses to heed them. Doubtless there can be a remorse of pride, disgust at having let oneself fall into a sin for which one ordinarily feels repulsion. This is "the world's remorse" (2 Cor. 7. 10) which produces death, because it leads to despair. Such was Cain's remorse. But there is also a remorse which is a gift of God, "supernatural remorse" (*ibid.*) which leads to true repentance and conversion. Repentance is sometimes produced by a grace acting wholly from within. It is often produced by a shock from without, an act of divine punishment or a threat uttered by someone appointed to do so in God's name.

Not all trials are punishments. We have seen the case in St John's Gospel of the man born blind whose infirmity was the consequence neither of his own sin nor of a sin of his parents. But there are also punishments stamped with the mark of the divine displeasure. Of this sort were the tribulations which fell upon the Israelites when, at the time of the Judges, they had strayed into idolatry. It is undeniable that the Protestant Reformation came as a punishment for the refusal by churchmen for centuries to undertake a thorough-going reform. This lamentable tearing apart of Christendom, the cause of so much blood and so many tears, was surely retribution for persistence in slackness, disorder and sin.

In individual lives it is more difficult to see things clearly. The distinction between a punishment and a trial may often be ill-defined. But there are occasions when the person concerned can make the distinction clearly and be grateful to God for being punished in respect of his possessions and his body rather than of his soul and his eternal destiny.

Even the punishments of the next world are chiefly meant as a deterrent. The fire of hell is indeed the revenge of the material creation for having been perverted from its true end and made to serve vanity, but it is above all a grave warning not to fall short of the true purpose of life. The thought of hell has been for countless souls an unassailable barrier preserving their charity at a moment of grievous temptation.

And, if purgatory is less well known to us, the thought of being deprived for a time of the sight of God can induce us to labour for our purification, to sorrow for the sins that here below we call unimportant and to correct our defects. The certainty that we have one day to present ourselves before the holiness of God and the fear of seeing ourselves thrust away provide an irreplaceable incentive in the spiritual life.

Finally, in a more general manner, the vision of the universe, with all the griefs it contains, gives us an idea of that stream of filth and blood constituted by sin, which from the first day of creation has fought against God's work, not to destroy it, which would be impossible, but to diminish it, defile it and tarnish its lustre. It needs nothing less than the divine wisdom to renew it and make it once for all a thing more lovely than it would have been if evil had not been permitted.

CHAPTER XI

THE BENEFITS OF EVIL:

REPARATION

That God should make use of evil, which is the fruit of sin,
to release man from sin is a proof of his wisdom and goodness. Nonetheless it contains a mystery. It is instinctive in
man, even in childhood, to seek the means of restoring the
balance that has been upset by wrongdoing in some privation
or suffering. Expiatory sacrifice is based on this instinct. But
it is particularly unnecessary to think of God as having need
of this reparation. He never has need of anything or anyone.
His infinite peace is not disturbed by the rebellion of the
sinner. It is at our human level that these matters have their
place. The sinner voluntarily accepts the consequences of the
disorder he has caused. It is a way of returning to order, of
showing his repentance and drawing down God's pardon.
Then again, as it is extremely rare for the punishment to
correspond exactly and obviously to the sin that has been
committed, acceptance of evil awakens in us the sense of the
solidarity of mankind, the need of others' assistance for our
own recovery, and the desire to help others to return to God.
In short, the fact of solidarity calls forth the virtue of charity.

It is important first of all to emphasize that it is not suffering as such which makes reparation, but suffering united

to love, suffering accepted by love, suffering as a proof of love.

> Know then, you sinners, that it is not enough to endure much; that although as a general rule those who suffer much in this life are right to hope for rest in the next, because of the hardness of our hearts this rule is not always obeyed. There are many on the cross who are far removed from the Crucified. The cross for some is a grace, for others a means of retribution. Of the two men on the cross with Jesus Christ, one found mercy there, the other the rigours of justice; one achieved his salvation, the other entered upon his damnation. The cross raised the patience of the one up to paradise and hurled the impenitence of the other down to hell. (Bossuet, *Sermon on Suffering*, Palm Sunday, 1661.)

This is what happened in a unique manner in the passion of the Son of God. He took human nature with its capacity for suffering. He had not deserved the slightest punishment for sin, since he was wholly innocent, without stain, separated from sinners and without a share in the solidarity of original sin. Nevertheless he took the place of Adam and made himself the head of sinful humanity in order that he might be able to act in the name of all men and extend his merits to them. Then, through love for his Father and for the brethren he had given himself by his Incarnation he went on his way to suffering and death.

The striking thing is the unheard-of profusion of humiliation and suffering with which he accomplished it. All his actions, as actions of the Son of God, were of infinite merit and value. Consequently the least suffering he accepted would have sufficed to redeem the world, the least humiliation he accepted would have put right the dislocation Adam's pride had caused in the world.

In fact he accepted the cross, the supreme humiliation. The New Testament hardly draws any attention to the physical sufferings of Christ, but a great deal to the ignominy of this type of death. For the Greeks and Romans it was the sentence of dishonour passed on the criminal slave, not to be mentioned among respectable people. One recalls the unfortunate Gavius crucified by Verres who kept on shouting, "I am a Roman citizen". For the Jews it was death "beyond the city gate" (Hebrews 13. 12), which publicized God's curse on the man who had been cut off from his people. "God's curse lies on the man who hangs on a gibbet" (Deut. 21. 23).

But although the evangelists and apostles do not insist on the sufferings of crucifixion, these sufferings nevertheless deserve our attention. As a matter of fact, the cross appears to be the most horrifying form of torture.

> Jesus did not cry out, but his face was horribly contorted. . . .
> His thumb began beating against the palm of his hand with
> a violent, imperious motion. His median nerve had been
> affected. . . . An indescribable pain spread like lightning
> through his fingers, leapt up to his shoulder like a streak of
> fire and burst in his neck. It is the most unbearable pain a man
> can endure, that produced by an injury to the main nerve-
> branches.
>
> . . . He was thirsty, his features were drawn. His haggard
> face was streaked with the blood which clotted all over it. His
> mouth was half-open and his lower lip already began to drop.
> A little saliva ran into his beard, mixed with the blood dripping
> from his flattened nose. His throat was dry and burning, but
> he could no longer swallow. He was thirsty.
>
> . . . . The muscles of his arms tightened of their own accord
> with a contraction that became more pronounced; his deltoids,
> his biceps were taut and jutting out. His fingers were bent like
> hooks. Such cramp! . . . Look now at the same unnatural rigid
> protrusions at his thighs and calves and his toes which are
> bent back. . . . it is what we call tetany, a generalized state of
> cramp. . . .

This is no imaginative description but a medical analysis of crucifixion made by Dr Pierre Barbet, surgeon at St Joseph's Hospital in Paris. We can understand the avowal he makes at the beginning of his study: "I consider that it requires heroic virtue, or else failure to understand, that it is necessary to be a saint, or unconscious, to perform the Stations of the Cross. For myself, I am unable to do it."[1]

Confronted with humiliations and sufferings such as these we cannot help asking why, since they were not absolutely necessary, Christ wished to undergo them. First, it can be replied that our Lord could not obtain pardon for men without the risk of demoralizing them, that is, without inducing them to minimize the seriousness of sin and blunting their sense of what God demands. Henceforth Christians would be able to read on the crucifix, as if from a living book, the ugliness, the disorder and the guilt of sin. If God's mercy is satisfied, his justice has remitted nothing of the punishment it imposed.

The second answer—which carries weight—is that for his Father and for us the horrifying suffering Christ endured is proof of his love. We could never have imagined how greatly God set store by our salvation and happiness if Christ had been content to save us by a lesser degree of humiliation and suffering. "He still loved those who were his own, whom he was leaving in the world, and he would give them the uttermost proof of his love" (John 13. 1). This is what the cross makes us realize. From the other aspect again, since the whole drama of sin consists in a refusal of love, the reparation made by suffering lies in its being an indication and proclamation of love.

What is true of Christ is true also, due allowance being made, of the Christian. We have quoted the words of St Paul: "In this mortal frame of mine, I help to pay off the debt which the afflictions of Christ leave still to be paid, for the sake

---

[1] Dr. P. Barbet. *La passion corporelle de Jésus.* Issoudun 1946. (English trans.: *The Corporal Passion of Christ*, Fresno, Calif., Academy Library.)

of his body, the Church" (Coloss. 1. 24: *cf.* above, Chapter V). What is "the debt which the afflictions of Christ leave still to be paid"? Nothing, if it refers to their merit and value for satisfaction. Everything, if it refers to our love. We cannot benefit from Christ's redemption, once we have reached the age of reason, without sharing in his love for his Father and his love for our brethren, without taking our share of his cross: "If any man has a mind to come my way, let him renounce self, and take up his cross daily, and follow me" (Luke 9. 23). Our Lord's cross is our cross. Simon of Cyrene as he carries our Lord's cross is the type of all of us. Christ offered our sufferings with his own to enable us to offer his with ours.

> So perfect a bond unites the least of his members with their crowned head, that the most unimportant sick person is enabled to reproduce on his own sick-bed the actual suffering of Jesus on the cross. This person on his own sick-bed reproduces literally, actually, effectively, our Lord's passion, his martyrdom, and that of the other saints and martyrs. . . . The least known sick person reproduces literally our Lord's passion, his prayers, his sufferings, his merits, and shares in the passion, the prayers, the sufferings, the virtues, the merits of our Lord; the sickness, prayers, sufferings, virtues, merits of the least known sick person on the one hand, and the passion, sufferings, virtues and merits of Jesus on the other, are paid into the same treasury.[2]

This close bond enables us to expiate our own sins and make reparation for those of others. We only make reparation for others, it is true, in virtue of merit *de congruo*. Only Christ can merit in justice for others, in virtue of his grace as head of the human race. But the contribution that our suffering makes to the restoration of order in a universe disrupted by sin is nonetheless a reality.

When love is lacking, when acceptance and resignation fail,

---

[2] Péguy, *Un nouveau théologien*, p. 28.

order is nevertheless restored by punishment. It is not God who suffers. His external glory is obtained by the punishment of crime as well as by the reward of merit. And if in the former case it is a lesser glory, it is compensated in the wisdom of God by the excess yield of merit of those who have suffered from evil, and from the wicked. We must not, however, forget that God only permits evil. His primary and persistent will is "that all men should be saved, and be led to recognize the truth" (1 Tim. 2. 4).

CHAPTER XII

THE BENEFITS OF EVIL:
THE PERFECTING POWER

We may now look at a further aspect of the mystery of evil. The Epistle to the Hebrews teaches us that it was by suffering that Christ was made perfect: "We can see one who was made a little lower than the angels, I mean Jesus, crowned, now, with glory and honour because of the death he underwent; in God's gracious design he was to taste death, and taste it on behalf of all. God is the last end of all things, the first beginning of all things; and it befitted his majesty that, in summoning all those sons of his to glory, he should *crown with suffering the life* of that Prince who was to lead them into salvation" (Hebrews 2. 9–10).

How can Christ be made perfect, when he himself *is* perfection? His human nature expresses, in a way suitable to our understanding and our degree, yet eminently and exactly, God's perfection. Nothing can be added to his grace and holiness. We can understand easily enough how we ourselves are formed and completed by suffering. But how can this hard apprenticeship, this school of sorrow, complete the perfection of Christ? Everything is his, nothing is outside his ken.

"What suffering gave him was a human experience of pain,

to make him complete in his rôle as head and high-priest of humanity."[1]

The Son of God did not become incarnate in an unimpaired humanity, but in a guilty humanity that had already tasted punishment. If humanity had been guiltless and free from suffering, he would not have had to experience the harsh lessons of endurance. But the humanity of which he is the head is this guilty and suffering body in which there is "no health anywhere, from sole to crown, nothing but wounds" (Isaias 1. 6). If Christ had passed through the world in joy and laughter he would not have been truly our brother, he would have had no comfort to offer us. "It is because he himself has been tried by suffering, that he has power to help us in the trials we undergo" (Hebrews 2. 18). Having taken mankind's burden and miseries upon himself he is "able to feel for them when they are ignorant and make mistakes, since he, too, is all beset with humiliations" (Hebrews 5. 2).

When we consider the passion of Christ we are necessarily saddened and humiliated since by our sins we were its cause: "It was for our sins he was wounded" (Isaias 53. 5). If there is anything to sweeten this sorrow it is the thought that for Christ suffering was the instrument of his greatness or, as Scripture has it, the crown of his life.

It is in this way, too, that his priesthood attains its fullness. "The purpose for which any high-priest is chosen from among his fellow-men, and made a representative of men in their dealings with God, is to offer gifts and sacrifices in expiation of their sins" (Hebrews 5. 1).

Other priests chosen from among men are sinners. They are obliged to offer sacrifices, first for their own sins, then for those of the people. Christ, on the other hand, did not take sin on himself, but took on himself the penalties and humilia-

[1] Jules Lebreton, S.J., *The Life and Teaching of Jesus Christ*, London, Burns Oates, and New York, Macmillan, 1956.

tions of sin and, on the day of his baptism, took his place in the ranks of sinners. And so "it is not as if our high priest was incapable of feeling for us in our humiliations" (Hebrews 4. 15). He is gentle and humble of heart. He has a welcome for all those who come to him, and his suffering, which is greater than any known to man, makes him the most perfect priest, the most pure before God and the most forgiving towards his brethren. It is not in his person, nor in his holiness, that our Lord is made perfect by suffering, but in his rôle as head and high priest of humanity.

His members will be perfected by suffering in a manner more or less complete in proportion to their sanctity and union with God. This is true first of all of our Lady. Her sanctity is without equal, since her vocation as Mother of God admits of no comparison. Immaculate in her conception, loaded with the most singular favours by God, she was prepared for her part by the Holy Ghost fashioning within her the tabernacle of the Most High. But she was not only the mother of the Son of God, she was also the mother of Christ our Redeemer, and that meant suffering for her, but brought her also a new perfection to make her more lovely in the eyes of God together with greater power of drawing men to herself.

Her suffering, inasmuch as she was perfectly innocent and had never known by experience what sin is, was bound to be the most bitter and profound suffering ever undergone. The old man Simeon made no mistake when he foretold that a sword of grief should pierce her soul.

See her at the street corner waiting for the treasure of all Poverty. Her eyes are tearless, her mouth is dry. She says not a word and watches Jesus come. She accepts. Once again she accepts. The cry is sternly repressed in the strong, close-guarded heart. She says not a word and watches Jesus Christ. The mother watches her Son and the Church her Redeemer. Her heart rushes violently towards him like the cry of a dying soldier. She stands upright before God and offers him her soul to read. There is nothing in her heart that refuses or draws back. No fibre of her transfixed heart but accepts and consents. And like God himself who is there, she is present. She accepts and watches this Son she has conceived in her womb. She says not a word and watches the Saint of saints. (Paul Claudel: *Chemin de la Croix*, 4th station.)

The poet was absolutely right to emphasize her acceptance. It is voluntary acceptance of suffering which brings perfection, because it is a sign of love and, in this case, of heroic love. It must never be forgotten that it is by charity that the soul is made perfect. Our Lady here is only continuing what has been the dominant note of her life. "Let it be unto me according to thy word" (Luke 1. 38). She accepted completely her vocation as mother of God and mother of the crucified Saviour. That is why Christ said of her "Blessed are those who hear the word of God, and keep it" (Luke 11. 28).

What is true of our Lady is true also of the saints. In the earliest period of the Church honour was paid to the martyrs, those, that is, who had set the seal to their love of God by fully accepted suffering and the sacrifice of their lives. They were looked upon as the true servants of Christ, because they had shared in his passion. "If anyone is to be my servant," our Lord said, "he must follow my way; so shall my servant too be where I am" (John 12. 26).

After them the confessors are given honour, those, that is, who have only been baulked of the martyr's crown by circumstances independent of their will, often men who have suffered for Christ, of whom it can be said, as of St Martin, "Although the persecutor's sword did not take away his life, he did not miss the palm of martyrdom" (Magnificat antiphon, November 11th). This outlook carried away a great number of men into the deserts. They wished to lead the life of angels by celibacy, the life of prophets by meditation on the word of God, and also to take the place of the martyrs whom the cessation of persecution had made more rare. They threw themselves bravely into combat with the devil and were ready for their Lord's sake to endure hunger, thirst, nakedness, persecution and unceasing temptations. They cannot be accused of masochism as if in suffering they were pursuing self-indulgence. They sought only to prove and increase their love.

One of the characteristic examples of the perfection which suffering wins for holy people is provided by St Joan of Arc. If the detestable trial at Rouen had not taken place, if Joan had ended an honourable career in a middle-class house on the outskirts of Orléans, we should have had a wonderful adventure, crowned at first by success, but partly discredited by successive reverses, we should have the memory of a devout, good and heroic woman, attentive to the poor, devoted to her military duty. Even if she had in fact been a saint it would have escaped most people's notice. As it is, we see her overborne by a bench of pedantic lawyers, strangers to human feeling, imprisoned for months in a foul cell, deprived of the Mass and communion which were her consolation, at times sick and nearly dying. We see her worst of all in despair, with the feeling that her voices had deceived her. "Now I believe only in God," she said. Next there is the stake which she feared so much, to which she went nevertheless with high courage, to die repeating over and over again the name of Jesus. Her heroic loyalty not only proved her love but also increased her stature indescribably. For all that she was put out of the way as seditious, cruel, an apostate, a schismatic, and the accusation corroborated by a process of condemnation which constitutes a wonder of jurisprudence, the trial has turned against the judges, the transparent clarity of Joan's replies has given us the secret of her soul which would otherwise have remained in obscurity, and the glory of the saints has crowned a life which, but for suffering, would have lacked any enduring brilliance.

Examples could be multiplied from the lives of the saints. It can be said with certainty that not one of them has attained the heroic perfection of sanctity except in and by suffering. Those who have endured the purifying agonies of the contemplative life have not been the least tried. Even those living in a Christian country, among people who shared their ideals and beliefs, have met with misunderstanding, persecution or grave illness.

We can now take our analysis a step further by examining the way in which Christians are perfected by suffering. In the first place it gives them a refinement in their relations with God, a concern for purity which they would never have had without the trials they have undergone. Many souls pass through most painful attacks of scruples once or several times during their lives. Without these scruples they would acquire the habit of acting in God's regard in a manner that, though correct, is dull and somewhat ill-mannered. There are those who are drawn by God to a higher way of life and a deeper mode of contemplation. As a rule they go through the most painful purifications, sometimes lasting a considerable time. This is the price of their progress in light and joy. Confronted with the holiness of God they realize his overwhelming demands and give themselves to him with an immeasurable increase of love.

Suffering also greatly increases love of our neighbour, at least in arresting the obstinate tendency to wall ourselves up in our own self-centredness. The suffering of others cannot be understood without personal suffering, I will go so far as to say, without a personal experience of suffering similar to that which calls for sympathy. Those who have never been ill do not realize the pain, the humiliation, the helplessness of the sick person they nurse; those who have never been tempted cannot imagine the feeling of instability and insecurity temptation brings with it; those whose hearts have never been weighed down with bitterness have no idea of what is endured by those deserted, despised or starved of love.

Love of God grows in a wonderful way as a result of suffering. It makes us understand how much we have been loved. "No one is so deeply touched by Christ's passion as he who has experienced like sufferings" (*Imitation of Christ*, II, 12. 4). It increases our confidence in the assurance that no one shares Christ's cross without being called to share his glory. It enables us to gain great merit, leading us to act solely for God, even in darkness, in pain, and when we feel God has abandoned us. Even purely human qualities are heightened, strengthened and made perfect by suffering. "There is something in suffering which makes us stronger, more manly, deeper: something which is the source of all heroism. Once we are touched by it, the mysterious power it contains grows stronger. By this means the child obtains the vitality of youth, the youth the gravity of the grown man, the grown man the strength of heroism, the hero the virtue of sanctity."[2]

In the supernatural world it is by trials, humiliations and persecutions that the soul receives its ultimate form, the ability to take the place prepared for it in the mystical body of Christ. The Vesper hymn for the feast of the Dedication of a Church gives magnificent utterance to this:

Tunsionibus, pressuris	Many a blow and biting sculpture
Expoliti lapides	Fashioned well those stones elect,
Suis coaptantur locis	In their places now compacted
Per manus artificis,	By the heavenly architect,
Disponuntur permansuri	Who therewith hath willed for ever
Sacris aedificiis.[3]	That his palace should be decked.

We can understand how it was that the author of the *Imitation* gave to one of his finest chapters the title "Of the Royal Road of the Holy Cross" (II, 12), and when we consider this transformation of suffering into holiness and glory, we recall the words of St Teresa of the Child Jesus, *"Souffrir passe, avoir souffert ne passe pas"*.[4]

[2] Donoso Cortès.

[3] Unknown author, 6–7th century; trans. J. M. Neale.

[4] "Suffering passes away, the experience of suffering never passes away."

CHAPTER XIII

COSMIC EVIL

One of the great difficulties in overcoming the problem of evil
arises from the fact that our conception of the universe is
no longer that of the Greeks, still less that represented by
the schematic accounts of the Bible. The Greeks thought of
a flat earth, circular in shape, surrounded by the river Ocean,
consisting of the three continents grouped around the Inner
Sea—the Mediterranean. Encircling the earth were concentric,
moving spheres, of incorruptible substance, the farthest being
the sphere of the fixed stars. The Hebrews thought of the
earth as supported on the lower waters. Above was the firma-
ment which supported the upper waters. It was held up by
the mountains as if by pillars. In either conception the universe, however vast, appeared on a human scale. It was the
earth which was its centre, and it was man who gave the
earth its importance. It can readily be imagined how all evil
was considered as the consequences of man's sin.

In the last few centuries the dimensions of the world have
expanded for us in an unprecedented degree and new discoveries make it, so to speak, grow larger every day. The
earth has lost its rôle as the centre of the universe. It is now
no more than one of the planets whose orbit turns around
the sun. But whereas the sun had itself taken the central
place after the Copernican revolution, we now know that it
is only a star in a universe whose dimensions are computed
in light-years, although we shall never be able to see its limits.

There is a possibility that it is expanding continually. These gigantic perspectives give us an infinitely higher idea of God's wisdom and power, but our conception of evil is altered at the same time. The saying of the Bible, "And God saw that it was all good", remains, to be sure, absolutely true. It is an essential part of what Christian teaching affirms. The world is the work of God, of God who is good, and no evil can come from him. However, when Genesis portrays evil as the consequences of man's sin, logically and chronologically subsequent to that sin, what was easy to admit when the sublunary world was thought to be corruptible and the heavenly world incorruptible is no longer plausible. Thanks to the analysis of the spectrum we now know that the world of the stars is no more glorious than our own. It is composed of the same elements, whose presence is detectable in all the stars. So it is in itself corruptible. Moreover science discloses many features existing before mankind which we used to consider part of the evil in the world.

There is something surprising in the considerable extent of emptiness in the universe and in the frantic dispersal of the heavenly bodies, which seems so unfavourable to the diffusion of the superior forms of being. Against this background it is difficult to think of life as more than a chance episode on a prodigious scale, out of harmony with the aims which are nature's ordinary concern. What is more, life itself is far from appearing in perfect harmony, when the amount of knowledge available is as great as it is today. The further it goes in the study of life, the more scientific knowledge feels obliged, side by side with the most magnificent developments, to see traces of poverty in nature, the manifestations of which involve cruelty, monstrosities and depravity. Still more disconcerting is the appearance, with sentient forms of life, of pain. It is the decisive indication, it seems, of a lack of harmony in being.[1]

[1] P. D. Dubarle, O.P., in *Theology Library*, Vol. II (ed. A. M. Henry, O.P.), Chicago, Fides and Cork, Mercier Press, 1957.

It appears, then, that sin began before man and prepared the way for man's own sin. This is what Genesis gives us to understand in introducing the mysterious serpent whose identity we are never told, but who from the start appears opposed to God and in command of the movements that resist God. "He, from the first, was a murderer"; from the beginning of man's existence (John 8. 44). It seems likely that he had already at an earlier time introduced disorder into the handiwork of God.

True enough, there is need for prudence in this kind of discussion as a safeguard against the mistakes of Manicheism. The devil is not a principle on an equal footing with God. He is God's creature, unable to act except in so far as God permits, and God makes use of the damage he causes in order to bring about a greater good and a more beautiful harmony. *Mirabiliter condidisti, mirabilius reformasti*: "You have created in a wonderful manner, you have re-created in a manner still more wonderful."[2] In any case it is certain that the history of the world did not begin with man, but that, at the very beginning, there took place a revolt of part of the angelic creation.

By man's complicity the devil had become the "Prince of this world." The phrase comes from Christ himself. For once the father of lies was almost speaking the truth when he offered our Lord the kingdoms of the world: "They have been made over to me, and I may give them to whomsoever I please" (Luke 4. 6).

To root out evil from the world Christ bravely set about fighting the devil. Christ is the "strong man, fully armed" (Luke 11. 21) who takes possession of the devil's stronghold. To be sure, mankind needed to be taught, to be healed, to be helped, but above all they needed to be rescued from the devil. It is the conclusion of the prayer he taught his apostles:

[2] *Leonine Sacramentary,* Collect of Christmas; *cf.* prayer at blessing of water in the Ordinary of the Mass.

"deliver us from the evil one" (Matthew 6. 13).[3] The contest seems to end with a complete victory for the devil who "returns with seven other spirits more wicked than himself". He inspired so much hatred against our Saviour that his enemies finally made away with him. But this is a mistaken view. "He who rules this world has had sentence passed on him already", he has "no hold over me" (John 16. 11; 14. 30). The victory won by Christ's obedience over the devil's rebellion is, through his resurrection, made once and for all an accomplished fact. But just as on a battlefield scattered elements often struggle on long after the decision has been obtained, so the devil imposes on the Church a struggle lasting until the end of time.

This is a fact we must not forget: the forces of evil which fight against the Church of God are intelligent and organized. There is a limit to what they can do, but they are nevertheless powerful and active. It is difficult to say whether they act only in the semi-conscious sphere of temptation, or whether they possess also a power of directing, or misdirecting, the course of the material world. But experience proves that they have at their command real and effective forces, to such an extent that the Church, which is a Church militant, that is, a body organized for battle, constantly has recourse to exorcisms when she makes use of the material elements. It is not only the body of the unbaptized person that she sees as the prey of the devil, but water, oil and salt. The devil is everywhere and, following the instruction of her first pontiff, she watches well, because the devil, who is her enemy, goes round about her roaring like a lion, to find his prey (Cf. 1 Peter 5. 8).

The Middle Ages, following the Fathers, St Augustine and St Gregory the Great in particular, delighted in somewhat grotesque and frightening diabolic imagery. From the time of the Renaissance people have been misled by the childishness of this imagery. It has been a factor in our losing the

[3] *Malo* is taken as masculine rather than neuter. (*Trans.*)

awareness of the devil and his power and we have difficulty
now in realizing that we are engaged in a gigantic struggle
in which the battlefield and the prize of victory is humanity
itself and the loyal agents fight side by side with Christ against
the devil and his angels. There is no doubt that the battle
is won already, but no one has the right to retire from it and
desert his brethren until such time as it is brought to an end
by the coming of Christ in glory. For Satan has his accom-
plices among men; his business is to put men to the test,
his ambition to bring about the fall of the greatest possible
number of them.

There is more in all this than the mere survival of popular
beliefs. Recent popes have recalled this hostile presence again
and again. Leo XIII caused private Masses to be followed by
a short formula of exorcism. Pius XII, speaking of the cam-
paigns at present being waged against the Church, said on
February 11th, 1949: "We consider, Venerable Brethren, that
this could not come about except for some machination of the
infernal spirit whose whole purpose is the hatred of God
and the injury of mankind."

So much we can see; to this extent the problem of evil
becomes clearer. It is not solved. The most penetrating minds
have failed to give a perfect and definitive solution to put
the soul at rest and banish suffering, fear and remorse.

In 1927 Bergson asked Jacques Chevalier certain questions
concerning the problem of evil. "I should like to know," he
said, "what becomes of the problem of evil for someone who
sees it from God's standpoint and no longer asks himself the
question, the problem having disappeared. He should, however, be able, by comparing this new vision with the one he
used to have, to throw light on the question for the man to
whom it is still a living issue. Let us take physical suffering,
mental suffering in all its forms—these are trials, I am told.
But there is something in me which protests, and yet, from

the standpoint I describe, there should be no room for protest."

His mind turns to the cosmic evil which we have been looking at in this chapter. "What is the reason for life; what is the reason for beings whose life is accompanied by suffering and constant struggle? For man, yes. It is to bring him back to God. But life? The mystic ignores these problems. But there must be a light to illuminate the philosopher, to give an impetus, a direction to thought transcending philosophical speculation and bringing us on to the level where our business is to appreciate that which exists. What are we quâ living beings? What does life do in fact? Prey on itself. These races are incapable of rising to the point from which it is possible to rise to God. This is part of the diversity, I am told, which is due to God's munificence. Doubtless munificence can explain suffering and the rest. But this is an opinion of philosophers. I imagine that a mystic would see this evil disappear, would see that evil was a part of the supreme good—but how?"

Jacques Chevalier put the question first to M. Pouget, a learned and open-minded Vincentian, then to the Prioress of the Carmel of Montmartre.

M. Pouget repeated the classical arguments: a created being cannot be infinite. God can only give himself to his creatures *ad modum recipientis*, according to their capacity. Even in glory our knowledge of God will not be perfect. We shall be inside the sacred enclosure, but we shall not see everything. Then he touched on the actual question of evil. "Physical evil can be found without mental evil, without unhappiness. Physical evil does not prevent my being mentally at peace. There are mental ills, but God's mercy is a great thing. Our ills are the woof on which God weaves his mercy . . . We make God too stern . . . It is peace of soul which is supreme, we are under God's rule: I do what I can and refer everything to God.

"Animal suffering? Their rate of production demands the existence of carnivorousness. But they are not dissatisfied with life. They do not realize that they are suffering. They simply suffer. Man measures the time of his suffering and at each moment he suffers his illness in its entirety. The animal's suffering is only momentary. It is man's greatness which makes him suffer ...

"Life is a force which thrusts forward wherever it finds matter capable of receiving it. It makes use of other beings ...

"Offences against God are always finite. They are more than compensated for by Christ's submission to God, which has an infinite value ..."

Bergson was greatly interested in M. Pouget's reply, particularly by what he had to say about animal suffering, which removed his difficulty.

The substance of the reply of the Prioress of Carmel was as follows: The mystic is equally unable to give an intellectual solution to this terrible problem. For him the solution of such a question is indirect, but certain nevertheless, in the sense that a higher, indescribably sure mode of knowledge of the omnipotence and infinite love of God, of his essential goodness and the sovereign order which we shall discover—so soon—in eternal life, constitutes for the mystic, not a direct, intelligible solution, but a certainty that this problem is resolved in the harmony and triumph of good.... "There is a transformation of suffering when it is allied to a kind of sublime joy, in the case of the mystic, or a cleaving to God's will, in the case of the simple Christian, a certainty which, with its full power of trust and love, takes the place of intellectual restlessness—how shall I put it?—with an evidence that is truly compelling. The intuitive knowledge which the soul has of God, of goodness and of love, is such that an inexpressible assurance replaces the questioning of the intellect." Bergson found this letter admirable.

The mystery persists, but it is one which the divine essence in its infinite goodness illuminates without destroying. We are half-way up the mountain on the shaded side, but on the other slope the sun has risen and already the sky is full of light.

CHAPTER XIV

THE FUTURE OF EVIL

Today a large section of humanity (carried away by Marxist ideals, believes with an iron assurance in the disappearance of evil: for the present the proletariat makes great sacrifices, endures hardships, devotes itself to a ferocious struggle, but the day will come when, with equality among men, peace, justice, liberty and, in short, happiness, will be established in so far as is compatible with the human condition. We may add that scientific progress will bring about a new degree of health and security so that sickness and death will be, so to speak, overcome. These prospects constitute a powerful reason for hope, and it often happens that Marxists reproach Christians with a refusal to share in it and with an attitude of resignation to earthly evil leaving it to God to restore the balance in heaven. Thus it is necessary to examine what faith teaches us about the future of evil.

It is a point on which Christian teaching is categorical: evil will persist throughout eternity. There will be evil spirits and damned souls who are separated from God for ever. Punishment, an evil which becomes in some measure a good by restoring the balance of justice, remains evil in itself. Great minds like Origen have gone astray in this matter. The Church has disowned them, despite the real sanctity of the great "didascalus" and the countless services he had rendered her. She was bound to preserve the deposit entrusted to her.

What then is our hope concerning evil? In simple terms, it is a theological hope, founded, not on our estimates and desires, but on the promises of God. First, God promises to give himself as the reward to those who seek him. Himself, that is, everything, the complete good which leaves nothing to be desired, beside which nothing can be counted, with which nothing can be compared. Then, since all other goods are only God's small change, the prelude to the enjoyment of God, they will be given into the bargain a new heaven and a new earth, that is, the glorification of matter. No sorrow, no bitterness will remain for the elect. God himself will wipe away all the tears from their eyes. Even the existence of the damned, seen in the peace of God, will no longer, properly speaking, be a cause of grief. Souls will no longer grieve for not having reached such a high degree of glory as they should, though perhaps that will have been one of their punishments in purgatory. God will not permit the least shadow of sorrow or regret to remain for his chosen. All will be wonderfully contented with what they possess.

God promises to give himself to us on earth, too. It is himself that he gives in sanctifying grace, and it is his action, light and power that he gives in actual grace. As for earthly goods, they are a foretaste of the riches of God and the joys of heaven. But God promises to give himself to us here only in an incomplete fashion, not in sight, but in faith. Consequently we can only enjoy him partially on earth. So there will always be a certain room for evil. Our Lord does not leave us ignorant of this. His servants will have to carry their cross every day and follow him. "All those who are resolved to lead a holy life in Christ Jesus," St Paul tells us, "will meet with persecution" (2 Tim. 3. 12).

To be sure, wherever the Gospel spreads, certain forms of suffering disappear. It is a gospel of peace, light and liberty. By liberating from sin it lightens the burden of the world. By spreading brotherly love it removes many ills and much affliction from the earth. But the propagation of the Gospel does not eliminate sin entirely. The great ages of faith have been ages also of great sinners, and sin always multiplies suffering. Then again, the more saints there are, the more souls are found undergoing the terrifying purifications of mysticism.

To what extent will the Gospel spread? We have no promise from God on this point. Our Lord assures us that his Gospel will be preached throughout the earth *in testimonium illis*, as a witness to them. He gives us no assurance that this will result in the conversion of the world. In fact he seems to say the opposite when he asks, "When the Son of Man comes, will he find faith left on the earth?" (Luke 18. 8). "When the Son of Man comes, all will be as it was in the days of Noe" (Matt. 24. 37).

The prophetic and apocalyptic writings agree in describing still more plainly the last days of the world as a time of bitter struggle, when Satan will marshal all the riches of his imagination to destroy the friends of God. In other words evil will persist right up to the end. Either the Apocalypse of St John is meaningless or it is evidence that Christians of every age will need comfort in persecution and when tempted by the devil.

It is possible there may be a certain respite in the persecution: "I saw, too, an angel come down from heaven, with the key of the abyss in his hand, and a great chain. He made prisoner of the dragon, serpent of the primal age, whom we call the devil, or Satan, and put him in bonds for a thousand years, thrusting him down to the abyss and locking him in there, and setting a seal over him. He was not to delude the world any more until the thousand years were over; then, for a short time, he is to be released" (Apoc. 20. 1–3).

It is important, however, to be on one's guard always against a naïve millenarianism such as has always been condemned by the Church, not as heretical, but as totally foreign to her thought. Even if the world over a long period came to bear the stamp of the Gospel in its institutions, it would not follow that all men were saints and their sins, like those of their forebears, would continue to weigh on the world. So long as the earth lasts happiness will be found only in poverty, resignation, tears, a burning desire for holiness, compassion for others, and the struggle for purity and peace. And when, after the final battle, the victory that has been Christ's ever since his death will be made completely manifest in its full extent, the world in which this happens will be a world renewed and glorified.

By temperament a Christian may be more or less of an optimist or more or less of a pessimist, but only within the limits marked out by revelation. Evil has a place in the universe defined by God's providence which it is unable to overstep. The wisdom of God makes use of this evil, and will do so until the end, for a greater good, and for Christians filled with the Spirit of Christ the struggle, more or less violent but always a reality, will remain a duty to the end.

PART IV

PRACTICAL CONCLUSIONS

CHAPTER XV

PREPARATION FOR

SUFFERING

The problem of evil raises a number of special problems for the human conscience. Should suffering be welcomed or thrust aside? Is it right to try to relieve those sufferings which are part of the condition of human existence and will never in any case disappear completely? Is it not opposing the divine plan to set oneself against suffering? Is not humanity impaired if it is deprived of one of its highest and most precious possessions? The solution of these various difficulties needs careful study. Two general principles emerge: first, suffering is an evil and is never to be sought for its own sake. Secondly, it is only a relative evil by comparison with sin, which is an absolute evil, and from this relative evil not only the wisdom of God, but also man's intelligence, can and should derive some good.

The first question to arise is that of the preparation for suffering. It is produced by what the ancients called *apatheia*, a Greek word from which the English word "apathy" is formed, but meaning something very different, namely, absence of passion or suffering. It was the ideal of the Stoics and the Neo-Platonists,[1] but it was taken up by the early

[1] "Why," asks Seneca, "should we not give the name of happiness to the condition of a soul that is free, noble, fearless and stable and

spiritual writers of the Eastern Church who wished to exclude the Stoic element of strain and pride and make *apatheia* the prelude to heaven and the incorruptibility of the saints.

It was Evagrius of Pontus who produced the most important theory of *apatheia*. He made contemplation the end of the spiritual life. But contemplation, he pointed out, is impossible without *apatheia*. "In order to perceive the place of God in us, the soul must rise above all thoughts that have to do with things: it will never reach its goal unless it strips itself of the passions which, through thought, bind it to perceptible objects. It will strip itself of the passions by means of the virtues, of simple thoughts by means of spiritual knowledge. It will leave this knowledge behind in its turn when it perceives that light which, at the time of prayer, forms the place of God."[2]

Apatheia produces charity, since it frees the soul from the memory of injuries and hatred. Even if it cannot prevent diabolical temptation, it makes possible a prayer free from distraction, peace of soul and a dreamlike tranquillity.

This doctrine of *apatheia* did not achieve a great degree of popularity in the west. On the one hand, not all the passions were thought to be evil, and on the other, to recall words of St Jerome, the result of suppressing all the passions would be to turn man either into a block of marble or into a god.

However, it remains true that we ought to avoid useless suffering by preserving tranquillity in our hearts and souls. In the first place, we should keep away from anything that excites the nervous system unnecessarily. In our western civilization it is already subjected to constant shocks from pictures, lighting, news and publicity. In the second place, we should expect suffering as a normal thing in the course of this earthly life. We can thus avoid illusions, lack of resigna-

has cast away all dread and all desire?" As for Plotinus, he sees especially in *apatheia* a method of imitating the divine calm. "If we said that likeness to God consisted for a soul in acting according to reason and thus avoiding passion, we should not be mistaken."
[2] Migne, *Patrologia Graeca*, 40, 1237.

tion and agony of mind. "I do not promise," our Lady said to St Bernadette, "to make you happy in this world, but in the next." Perfect happiness is not for this life, although there is a real beginning of happiness for a man who loves God and submits to his will.

Next, we should acquire the habit of perfect freedom of mind by detachment from unnecessary things and by taking care not to mistake means for ends or helpful and pleasant means for necessary ones. It is certain that the virtue of poverty makes life a great deal easier.

Finally, following St Paul's example, we should not cling too much to our life here on earth: "I do not count my life precious compared with my work," he said to the Christians of Ephesus when going up to Jerusalem where he was to be arrested (Acts 20. 24).

All this will not enable us to be completely free from suffering—that is neither possible nor desirable—but we shall avoid unwholesome suffering and unnecessary pain. It does not need much experience for us to see that it is these which form the most important part of our earthly ills. To be sensible and reasonable is to spare oneself a host of worries, anxieties and pain.

This reasonable attitude should not, however, degenerate into hardness of heart or lack of feeling. Man is a partly spiritual, partly material being; his place is on the frontier of two worlds. Feeling, made conscious and spiritually interpreted, is an integral part of his being. To wish to renounce it would be to do violence to the harmony and beauty of the world.

CHAPTER XVI

RELIEVING THE

SUFFERING OF OTHERS

When men outside the Church accuse us of lack of interest in the present world and of neglecting to come to the help of those suffering here and now, they are flying in the face of history. There is evidence from every age of the care taken by real Christians, and by the saints particularly, to come to the aid of all those in distress. Our Lord's teaching makes it clear: "Blessed are the merciful; they shall obtain mercy" (Matthew 5. 7).

To be sure, there is always too much to do. As Péguy writes:

> Do what we may, do what we may, they will always go faster than we can. They will always do more than we do, more than we can. It takes no more than a spark to set fire to a farm. It takes, it has taken, years to build it up. That's easy, there's no catch in that. It takes months and months, it has taken work and more work to produce a harvest. It takes no more than a spark to send up a harvest in flames. It takes years and years to rear a man; it needed bread and more bread to feed him, and work and more work and work of every kind. And a single blow is enough to kill a man.... It is the business of a plough to work for twenty years, and it is the business of a sword to work for one minute and to emerge the stronger.[1]

[1] Péguy, *Le Mystère de la Charité de Jeanne d'Arc*, p. 24.

In spite of all that it is not necessary to have a ready-made solution to the world's misery. First of all we should try to understand it. Sometimes, when nothing more can be done, something is achieved simply by listening to the sorrows of the person who is suffering and letting him know that one is listening and is interested in him and accepts a share of what he is enduring. St Margaret Mary recalls in her memoirs that she had had two whitlows, one after the other. "I only really suffered anything from the first," she said. "Someone noticed the second and sympathized with me about it."

But we must aim at doing more, at bringing some real relief. Clearly this must be done with discretion. It is ill service to a child to let him off the hard work necessary for his studies and his education. But as a general rule suffering calls for our assistance. It must, however, be emphasized that it is more useful to put an end to unhappiness at its source than to relieve a particular case of suffering. It is more worthwhile to provide permanent employment than to make a temporary distribution of bread. To help a particular social class to obtain a secure and honourable way of life is a great deal better than giving away sums of money, however vast.

Such considerations could be prolonged endlessly. What is important is to remember that, although one can voluntarily resign oneself to one's own suffering, it can never be right to be resigned to the suffering of others.

CHAPTER XVII

RELIEVING ONE'S OWN
SUFFERING

Many problems of conscience arise here. We have seen the very real benefits that come from suffering. But today medical science has put at the disposal of all a wide range of products which allow pain to be suppressed without damage to the organism. Various tranquillizers come to mind, methods of analgesia, antenatal exercises and suggestion which produce a practically painless childbirth. To what degree is it permissible for the Christian to use these medicines or methods?

In several allocutions, Pius XII replied to this case of conscience. On January 8th, 1956, when asked whether, in virtue of the text of Scripture, "With pangs thou shalt give birth to children" (Gen. 3. 16), a mother was bound to accept all the suffering and to refuse analgesia obtained by natural or artificial means, the pope replied that there existed no obligation of this kind. "Even after the fall," he said, "man retains the right to make himself master of the forces of nature, to utilize them for his own advantage and, accordingly, to put to use all the resources nature has to offer to avoid or suppress physical pain" (*Acta Apostolicae Sedis*, 1956, p. 92).

On February 24th, 1957, he returned to the same question and indicated the motives for which it is permissible to avoid physical pain without conflicting with any serious obligation or with the ideal of the Christian life. "A great number of motives could be listed; but despite their diversity they come back in the end to the fact that, in the long run, pain hinders us from obtaining certain good things and impedes our higher interests. It may be that it is preferable for a particular person in a particular concrete situation, but in general the disorder it provokes forces men to defend themselves against it; doubtless it will never be eliminated from humanity completely, but its harmful effects can be kept within narrow limits" (ibid., 1957, p. 136).

Pius XII includes amongst these advantages and higher interests the need to perform surgical operations in the essential conditions of calm, rest and relaxation indispensable to the precision and safety of every movement of surgery. It goes without saying that peace of mind necessary for work, removal of temptations to anger and revolt against God's will, and relaxation of the body which facilitates prayer and a more generous self-giving, can also be valid reasons for using medicines and different kinds of tranquillizing treatment.

On the other hand, it is not permissible to refuse pain when it is evidence of the profession of faith, as it was in the case of the martyrs. The same is true of every occasion when a man is given the unavoidable alternative of enduring suffering or transgressing a moral duty by act or omission. And the pope recalls that "there have been, in our own generation, magnificent examples of Christians, who, for weeks, months and even years, have borne pain and physical violence in order to remain faithful to God and their conscience" (ibid., p. 134).

CHAPTER XVIII

ACCEPTANCE OF

UNAVOIDABLE SUFFERING

"When a Christian day after day, from morning to evening, performs all the duties imposed by his state, his profession, the commandments of God and men, when he prays with recollection, works with all his energy, resists his evil passions, shows towards his neighbour the charity and self-sacrifice due to him, bears without complaint all God sends him; his life is always under the sign of the cross of Christ" (Pius XII, *Acta Apostolicae Sedis*, 1957, p. 136).

There is in every Christian life a large measure of unavoidable suffering. First of all there is our daily work which in our civilization has assumed a considerable degree of importance. The value of contemplation is ignored, that of production exaggerated. But we cannot abandon our civilization whatever its failings. So we are caught up in work as though in the cogs of some factory machinery. The more of it we do, the more we find we have to do. However much we love our work, the wish to do it regularly, conscientiously, and in a manner on which other people can safely depend, can present us with a number of difficulties, and it is impossible without careful watch over oneself and a certain degree of suffering.

There occur also in every serious attempt to live a moral life a host of temptations which can only be overcome with a struggle: temptations to impurity, avarice or pride. In a world like ours in which so many people think only of "getting on", of making money and enjoying varied and continual pleasures, the maintenance of one's integrity, chastity and a modesty proper to one's state and talents, can become extremely hard, and it would be self-deception to refuse to recognize the fact.

It is impossible to forget bereavements, separations, and the crowd of griefs that they involve. Families arise only to break up as the children on reaching maturity choose a state of life, either in consecration to God's service or in marriage. Many large families end in the loneliness of two old people. There are also premature deaths, unforeseeable illnesss, hereditary defects that can suddenly reappear after having been forgotten for generations. Everyone has his cross to carry, through no choice of his own, fitted nevertheless to his capacity, accompanied by the grace necessary for bearing it even while he feels it and suffers from it.

What gives all this its spiritual value is not the suffering as such, but the love of God's will with which it is accepted and endured. "Acceptance of pain is only one way amongst many others of signifying that which is essential, the will to love God and serve him in everything. It is in the perfection of this disposition of the will that the quality and heroism of the Christian life first and foremost consists" (ibid., p. 136).

And, because there is often more love in obedience than in sacrifice, in acceptance of suffering imposed by circumstances than in suffering imposed on oneself, it can be said that acceptance of suffering constitutes a more indispensable means to perfection than suffering deliberately sought. Old spiritual writers were fond of saying: "By mortification you go to God on foot, by the cross that you accept you go to him on horseback."

CHAPTER XIX

SELF-IMPOSED SUFFERING

However valuable the cross that God imposes, it remains a fact that a truly Christian life includes some degree of voluntary mortification and we cannot condemn those who seek the growth of their spiritual life in voluntary suffering, provided it is for the love of God. For the Christian, suffering is bound up with the religious values and high ideals which enable it to be sought, not in order to beat records or for selfish motives, but to increase in charity, to expiate one's own sins and those of sinners and to purify oneself from the least imperfection.

"The life and sufferings of our Saviour," said Pius XII also on January 8th, 1956, "the pain so many great men have endured and sought out, as a result of which their maturity and development have reached the very summits of Christian heroism, the examples of resigned acceptance of the cross which we have before our eyes, all these reveal the meaning of suffering, of patient acceptance of pain in the day to day economy of salvation, during the time of this earthly life" (*Acta Apostolicae Sedis*, 1956, p. 92).

This is echoed in the whole spiritual tradition of the Church. It is enough to recall the place accorded to mortification by so many of the saints. It is possible, certainly, that in certain ascetic environments there has been a tendency to run after records analogous to that which appears in the world of sport. This way of seeking self could not lead either to peace or liberty of soul or, least of all, to God. It is nonetheless true that the saints have sought God in mortification, at times of a most severe nature, and have indeed found him.

Several times Pius XII reminds us of the example of our Lord who at the moment of his crucifixion was offered a cup of wine mixed with myrrh, which could have made him drowsy and dulled his perception, thus mitigating his pain. To show that he appreciated the act of the men or women who had prepared this drink, Jesus tasted it, but preferred not to drink it. The final moments of his agony were too precious and he was unwilling to lose any of his lucidity. The same thing applies, due allowance being made, to the Christian. When he reaches his last moments, the culmination of his sacrifice, then it is that he most surely bears the mark of the cross of Christ. He need not be reproached if he asks for or accepts drugs to make his passage easier, but one can also understand—and this would be the more perfect way—his not wishing to lose anything of those tremendous moments, and insisting on trying right up to the end to grow, maybe with a superhuman growth, in love.

This word, love, could form a summary of the whole doctrine of evil. In the last resort, God has permitted evil in order to be able, in a tragic manner that admits of no contradiction, to show his love for us by accepting our punishment and our suffering. Moreover, if suffering is in itself mere nothingness, it gains all its meaning from the fact that its acceptance becomes for us the means of proving and increasing the love we have for God and our neighbour.

SELECT BIBLIOGRAPHY

(An asterisk denotes works by non-Catholics)

HENRY, A. M., O.P. (Editor): *God and His Creation* and *Man and His Happiness,* Volumes 2 and 3 in the Theology Library, Cork, Mercier Press, and Chicago, Fides, 1956 and 1957.

† LEBRETON, Jules, S.J.: *Life and Teaching of Jesus Christ*, London, Burns Oates, and New York, Macmillan, 1956.

*LEWIS, C. S.: *The Problem of Pain*, London, Bles, and New York, Macmillan, 1945.

MARMION, Columba, O.S.B.: *Suffering with Christ*, Westminster, Md, Newman Press, 1952.

SIWEK, Paul, S.J.: *The Philosophy of Evil*, New York, Ronald Press, 1951.

WEBB, Bruno, O.S.B.: *Why does God permit Evil?* London, Bloomsbury Publications, 1959.

The Twentieth Century Encyclopedia of Catholicism

The number of each volume indicates its place in the over-all series and not the order of appearance.

All titles are subject to change.